"In this terrific book Moose t _____ ısary
to be a complete player. But ı _____ ın
technique—you need heart. My definition of heart is the desire,
passion, and will to be the very best. My friend Daryl has heart."

—Emmitt Smith, former Dallas Cowboy running back

"Obviously Daryl did more than just block for Troy and Emmitt
during his eleven-year NFL career—he became a student of the
game. A great read to get ready for an NFL Sunday at home or at
the stadium."

—Ed Goren, president, Fox Sports

"Daryl Johnston has written the complete encyclopedia of professional football. It's both an explanation and a celebration of the
game we love."

—Dick Stockton, Fox sportscaster

"I don't know that there is a more appropriate person to explain
the nuances of watching—and appreciating—the NFL game on
television than Daryl Johnston. As a player who enjoyed a very
productive and rewarding career with the Dallas Cowboys, Daryl
was an astute student of the game who thrived on preparation and
execution. That professional dedication has followed him to the
broadcasting booth where he has ascended to a level of success
that mirrors his days as a player. This book will effectively allow
the casual football viewer to earn a much greater understanding
of what is happening down on the field. It will also give the seri-
ous viewer a higher level of respect and appreciation for the
game, the men who play it, and the people who present it to the
millions of fans who watch NFL football every week."

—Jerry Jones, owner and general manager, Dallas Cowboys

Watching Football

Discovering the Game within the Game

Daryl Johnston
with **Jim Gigliotti**

INSIDERS' GUIDE®

GUILFORD, CONNECTICUT
AN IMPRINT OF THE GLOBE PEQUOT PRESS

Special thanks to Ron St. Angelo, Dallas, for his photography.
Text design: Casey Shain

Library of Congress Cataloging-in-Publication Data
Johnston, Daryl.
    Watching football: discovering the game within the game / Daryl Johnston
with Jim Gigliotti. –1st ed.
        p. cm.
    Includes index.
    ISBN 0-7627-3906-1
1. Football. I. Gigliotti, Jim. II. Title.
    GV950.6.J64 2006
    796.332–dc22

                                                                2005013173

Manufactured in the United States of America
First Edition/First Printing

Dedication

To my wife, Diane: Thank you for being there for me at every turn. You were thrust into the lifestyle of an NFL player and never waivered. You were there with me during the good times, but more important than that, you were there for me during the tough times. I love you!

Daryl

To Wendy, who opens my eyes to new wonders every day.

Jim

It started Friday afternoon and slowly progressed until Sunday. The game face. I was not the nicest person to be around during this transformation.

Photo by Ron St. Angelo

Contents

Acknowledgments

As a boy I played almost every sport, but I was always drawn to the game of football. It is a great game that teaches you valuable lessons that you can use in everyday life.

Thank you to all the players who came before me who helped make football America's favorite team sport.

To all my coaches and teammates, thank you for your contributions and help throughout my career.

And to my family, thank you for your support at every level at which I played this game.

I hope this book provides insight and appreciation for what I believe to be the greatest team game of all, the game of football.

Daryl Johnston

I've been watching football for a lot of years now, but never received quite the education that I did during the 2004 season. That year, thanks to the marvels of NFL Sunday Ticket, I reaped the benefits of Daryl Johnston's insightful analysis for all seventeen weeks of the regular season. Combine that with our weekly talks about the game, and I learned that there was a whole lot I had to learn. I'd like to thank Daryl for his great patience, good humor, and thoughtful answers to even the most basic questions I had for him in each conversation.

Thanks also to Jim Buckley of the Shoreline Publishing Group in Santa Barbara, California, for helping to kick off this project. And to editors Mary Norris and Julie Marsh of Globe Pequot Press for following through on it. I'm grateful also for the patient assistance of Mike McCord, the respected equipment manager of the Dallas Cowboys, for clarifying numerous issues relative to a player's gear.

Jim Gigliotti

The game of football is both physically and mentally exhausting. But from series to series and game to game, I couldn't wait to get back on the field.

Photo by Ron St. Angelo

The Game within the Game

"Keep your eye on the ball." How many times did we all hear that playing sports while growing up? And when we watch a football game from the stands or on television, what do we do? We all pretty much keep our eye on the ball.

We all see the quarterback hand off the ball to the running back and the linebacker make the tackle. Or we watch the quarterback fire a pass to the sideline as the cornerback reaches in to bat the ball away. Or we look at the kicker and follow the path of the ball as it goes through the uprights for a field goal.

But there are twenty-two guys who are in on each play during a football game. And, unlike just about every other team sport, none of those players can act alone. Every one of them has to rely on each of his teammates on the field to work in unison in order for a play to be successful. That's what makes football such a unique sport.

So, while we're all keeping our eye on the ball, what goes on every time the ball is snapped? Why is it important for the fullback to know what route the tight end is running? What is the defensive end doing when he loops behind the defensive tackle instead of taking the most direct path to the passer? And what is the wide receiver supposed to be doing on a running play?

Well, we're here to help.

I've been a color analyst for NFL games on Fox television since the 2001 season. But before that I played eleven years as a fullback for the Dallas Cowboys, beginning in 1989. I've seen the game from both sides—on the field and in the stands or on television. I don't really think of myself as being a member of the media. I think I can

Center Mark Stepnoski (53) and I made the walk down the tunnel at Texas Stadium together many times. I never took for granted how privileged I was to make that trek.

Photo by Ron St. Angelo

relate to the players out on the field more as a former football player. But I only retired in June 2000, still a relatively short time ago. And as I go along, fewer players will know me as a former player, so the way we relate to one another will change.

But for now, I still feel like a former player. I've been criticized in some circles for not being tough enough on the air. But I've been there, and I know that everyone who has ever played the game has been knocked on his behind now and then. So, unless a player has done something wrong or unethical, I don't get on him. Now, if some guy has done something for which I feel he deserves to get kicked out of a game, then I will get on my soapbox.

Watching Football is another kind of soapbox for me. It gives me a chance to talk to you, the reader—but also a viewer of football games—about what goes on during the course of a game. It is not intended to teach you how to play football. You won't find any practice drills in here, and it's certainly not an NFL playbook. But, if you want to know why the head coach went for it on fourth and 1, what the quarterback is doing when he yells "Red!" at the line of scrimmage, or just what on earth a zone blitz really is, then read on.

My goal here is the same as it is on every telecast that I work. When it's over, I hope the folks in the audience can say, "Wow, I really learned something there."

I don't think any sport can match the intensity and emotion that exists on a football field. Just ask Matt Vanderbeek.

Photo by Ron St. Angelo

PART ONE

Football
101

This may look like a simple huddle, but unique bonds are formed between teammates who take the field together. In Dallas it became our second family.

Photo by Ron St. Angelo

CHAPTER ONE

Inside Football

Looking Deeper into Football

They say that football is a descendant of soccer and rugby. But the version that has evolved over the past one hundred–plus years in the United States is a distinctly American game that inspires a religious fervor among its followers. I can tell you from experience that the passion and loyalty of football fans is unequaled by those of any other sport in this country. Football is the number one spectator sport in the United States.

I played pro football in Texas. And while they say everything is big in Texas, football is *really* big. And it's not just NFL football. The passion of Texas football fans starts with Friday night games in high school and continues with college games on Saturday and NFL games on Sunday and Monday.

The National Football League

By almost any statistical measure, the NFL tops the list of America's favorite sports leagues. I was fortunate enough to play in the NFL from 1989 until 1999. Every weekend from September through December, fans crammed stadiums to watch the Dallas Cowboys, "America's Team." But it was the same for everyone else around the country, too. More than one million people attend NFL games each weekend. And another one hundred million–plus watch NFL games on television.

As you might expect, most of the viewers are men. But it may surprise you that statistics also show that just about four in ten fans at

Game day is not just for players. Fans pack stadiums across the country to be a part of America's number one spectator sport.

Photo by Ron St. Angelo

NFL games are female, and that more than thirty million women watch pro football on television each weekend.

International Growth

I guess what I'm trying to say is, the game has become an integral part of life for a whole lot of people. And it's not just in this country, either. All around the world, more and more people are tuning in to football games.

In addition to weekly programming and live telecasts, the NFL has exported its product abroad with the American Bowl, a series of pre-season games that since 1986 have been played in cities around the globe, and with NFL Europe, a six-team spring league centered in Germany. Numerous youth programs have been initiated in countries around the world.

When I was with the Cowboys, we played preseason games in London, Tokyo, Mexico City, and Monterrey, Mexico. The two games in Mexico City each drew more than 100,000 fans!

*The calm before the storm . . .
Poised just inches from each
other, along the line of scrimmage, the Cowboys and the
Minnesota Vikings await the
snap of the ball.*

Photo by Ron St. Angelo

CHAPTER TWO

The Basics

A Complex Game

Football is a complex game, but the basics of the sport are easy to understand. If you're already tuning into NFL games on television, you're probably somewhat familiar with the primary rules. But if you're new to the game, we'll start with an abbreviated version of Football 101.

At its most basic the goal in football is to score more points than the opposition. That's how games are won—or lost. Points are accumulated by scoring a touchdown (6 points), kicking a field goal (3 points), or, in rarer instances, recording a safety (2 points). After scoring a touchdown teams also have the option of attempting a kick (for 1 point) or running or passing from scrimmage (for 2 points).

Gridiron Glossary

Scoring Terms

A player scores a **touchdown** when he runs into or gains possession of the ball in the opposing team's **end zone**—the area 10 yards deep at either end of the field of play. It's a score when the ball, in the control of a player, breaks the plane of the goal line.

A **field goal** is a kicked ball that goes between the uprights of the goalpost and over the crossbar. A **safety** generally occurs when a ballcarrier or passer is tackled in his own end zone.

Who Has the Ball?

The original football was almost round. Now they call it a "prolate spheroid." The ball gradually was tapered until the 1930s, when it was set at 11 to 11¼ inches long, 21¼ to 21½ inches around the middle, and 14 to 15 ounces in weight. Its unique shape results in unpredictable bounces that often contribute to the excitement of a game.

Offense

The offense is the unit of players in possession of the ball. Its primary responsibility is to advance the football by running or throwing it down the field, with its ultimate objective being to score a touchdown. Because an offense's quarterbacks, running backs, and wide receivers usually are the ones in possession of the football, these tend to be football's "glamour" positions and gain the most notoriety.

Defense

The defense is the unit charged with protecting a team's end zone. Its job is to stop the opposing team's offense from advancing the ball and forcing it to give up possession. Though generally it is the offense that scores points and the defense that prevents them, football's best defenses give their teams a boost by becoming adept at taking the ball away from the offense by intercepting passes or recovering fumbles. A good defense can return those "takeaways" for touchdowns or put its team's offense in position to score.

Special Teams

These are the kicking, kick-return, and kick-coverage units. Though they're on the field far less than their counterparts on offense or defense, special teams often have a direct influence on the outcome of the game. In particular, games can be decided by a single field-goal attempt in the closing seconds or in overtime.

Four Downs, 10 Yards

Football is played by teams of eleven players on each side on a field
that is 100 yards long, with an additional area called the end zone that
is 10 yards deep at both ends. Teams alternate possession of the football, with each side given four downs, or plays, to advance the ball 10
yards. A down is a play that begins with the snap of the ball and ends
when the ballcarrier is tackled, scores, or steps out of bounds, or when
a forward pass falls incomplete. It can be a running play, a passing
play, or an element of the kicking game like a punt or field-goal
attempt. Once a team makes the requisite 10 yards, it's awarded a *first
down,* and the four-down cycle starts again. A team maintains possession until it fails to make 10 yards in four downs, until a play results in
a score, until time runs out in either of a game's thirty-minute halves
(each half is divided into fifteen-minute quarters), or until the opponent takes away the ball.

Interceptions and Fumbles

When a defensive player catches a pass intended for an offensive
player, it's called an interception. A fumble occurs when an offensive
player loses possession of the ball before he is ruled down. He is
ruled down when any part of his body other than his hands makes
contact with the ground. When a defensive player picks up or falls on
a fumble, gaining possession of the ball, it's a fumble recovery.
Fumbles can be difficult for an official to determine because when
the ball comes loose in a pile of players, it's not always clear whether

the fumble or the end of the play came first. If a runner is ruled down by contact when he is in possession of the ball, the play is over and there can be no fumble.

Timing

Every game is sixty minutes of playing time, divided equally into four fifteen-minute quarters. The first two quarters make up the first half; the next two quarters the second half. Teams switch ends of the field after each quarter, with play continuing from the previous yard line at the conclusion of the first and third quarters. After the second quarter ends, there's a twelve-minute halftime, then the second half begins with a kickoff.

The clock is not a running clock. Factor in clock stoppages, halftime, time-outs, and so on, and a typical NFL game takes just about three hours to complete. College games typically take longer because of different rules about when the clock starts and stops and a longer halftime period.

Overtime

If a regular-season NFL game is tied at the end of four quarters, the teams play a "sudden-death" overtime—the team that scores first in any fashion wins. If no one scores after fifteen minutes of playing time (the equivalent of another full quarter), the game ends in a tie. Postseason games, however, can't end in a tie. Someone has to emerge a winner to advance to the next round or win the championship. So teams continue playing until one team scores. In college football overtime is different. Each team is guaranteed the same number of possessions beginning with a first down at their opponent's 25 yard line. The first team to outscore the other team in a given round of possessions wins.

That's it. That's the least you need to know to sit down in front of the television and have some sort of an idea what's going on. We'll explore the different phases of the game—offense, defense, and special teams—and the player positions for each later on.

Clock Stops and Starts

Specific rules govern when the game clock stops and starts. Here are a few of the most common in the NFL. The clock always runs (counting down from fifteen minutes to zero)

- on plays from scrimmage,
- when a ballcarrier is tackled in bounds on a play that doesn't result in a change of possession,
- on kickoffs (from the moment the ball is touched legally by any player in the field of play; on a kickoff that is returned out of the end zone, the clock starts when the kick returner crosses the goal line), and
- on punts and field goals.

It always stops

- on changes of possession,
- after any score or field-goal try,
- on incomplete passes,
- during any point-after try (kick, pass, or run),
- for time-outs, and
- at the two-minute warning.

If a ballcarrier goes out of bounds with more than two minutes left in the first half or more than five minutes left in the second half, the clock is stopped long enough for officials to spot the ball, then it's started again (inside of two minutes of the first half or five minutes of the second half, it stops until the next snap).

History Book

The longest NFL game ever played was on Christmas Day in 1971, when the Miami Dolphins and Kansas City Chiefs battled for 82 minutes, 40 seconds in an AFC divisional playoff game. The Dolphins finally prevailed 27–24 on a field goal midway through the second overtime period.

Every NFL player should have the opportunity to play at Green Bay's Lambeau Field. The history of the franchise and the atmosphere inside the stadium make it a truly unique experience.

Photo by Ron St. Angelo

The Field

The Battlefield

While it's unquestionably an exaggeration compared to the situation in which our troops find themselves, football borrows its vernacular from the language of combat: Quarterbacks throw the "bomb" (a long pass), offensive linemen engage one another in the "trenches" (along the line of scrimmage), and defensive players "sack" the passer (tackle him for a loss). The playing surface, then, is their battlefield. But it's unlike any battlefield you've ever seen. It has specific dimensions, markings, and boundaries. If you prefer, think of it as a chessboard—an appropriate analogy given the strategic nature of football.

Dimensions

The football field stretches 100 yards from goal line to goal line, with an end zone an additional 10 yards deep at each end. The field is a little more than half as wide—53⅓ yards, or 160 feet—as it is long. The 100-yard field was established at the initial college rules convention way back in the 1870s. In American football's formative years, the college game set the rules. When the pro game came along late in the nineteenth century, it generally followed those rules until the 1930s.

Many football fields have a "crown" to them. That is, if you stand on one side of the field and look across to the other side, you'll notice that it's not completely flat. The surface rises a bit toward the center of the field, then goes back down again toward the opposite sideline. This crown helps water drain off the field. Modern technology, though, has helped make crowns far less extreme.

The goal line is the field stripe that players must reach or cross to score a touchdown. It separates the end zone from the field of play and is considered part of the end zone. Every 5 yards on the field is noted by a white stripe that spans from sideline to sideline. Within each 5-yard stripe are four pairs of short stripes, called hash marks, which denote 1-yard increments and help officials position the ball for each play. Alternating 5-yard stripes also are identified numerically in increments of 10 up to 50 (midfield) and back down to 10. A small stripe in the middle of the field at the 2 yard line denotes the spot from which conversion plays are snapped.

Football players become so attuned to the dimensions of their work space that any variation is noticeable. In the late 1960s Dallas assistant coach Raymond Berry, a Pro Football Hall of Fame wide receiver in his playing days with the Baltimore Colts, reportedly felt something was wrong with the practice field at the Cowboys' training camp in Thousand Oaks, California. He took out a measuring tape, marched off the dimensions, and found that the field was 54 inches too narrow.

The boundary of the long axis of the field is called the **sideline** and includes a 35-yard area in which players and coaches must stand. The **end lines,** parallel to and 10 yards behind the goal line, mark the boundary on the short axis of the field. The entire area is rimmed by a white border 6 feet wide.

As I noted, the **hash marks** are the small white lines that denote 1-yard increments and are 18 feet apart on the right and left sides of the field. But they're important not only because they let you track yardage, but also because every play begins between the hash marks. If a ballcarrier is tackled inside the hash marks, the next play is snapped from that point. If he's stopped outside them, or if he goes out of bounds, the ball is brought to the hash mark on that side of the field. Hash marks are set 70 feet, 9 inches in from each sideline. They've gradually moved closer to the center of the field since originally being placed 30 feet from the sidelines back in the 1930s.

One thing that you won't see if you're at the game is the bold, **yellow field line** that shows up on television. The line stretches

History Book

The only NFL game ever played on a field of any other dimension than the normal 100-yard field was the season finale between the Chicago Bears and Portsmouth Spartans in 1932—and it turned out to be one of the most influential games in NFL history. The game was added to the end of the season because Chicago and Portsmouth had tied atop the league standings when the slate of regularly scheduled games was completed, and the league office wanted to crown an undisputed champion. When a blizzard forced the game indoors, the makeup of Chicago Stadium limited the playing field to only 80 yards (after teams crossed midfield, they were moved back 20 yards, in effect making it a 100-yard field). But the field also was too narrow (by 15 feet) and surrounded by hockey boards. So, when a play ended too close to the boards, the ball was brought in 10 yards toward the middle of the field for the next snap. That proved to make so much sense that it was adopted as a league rule the next year.

Chicago went on to win that 1932 game 9–0, with the key play a controversial touchdown pass from Bronko Nagurski to Red Grange. At the time all passes had to be attempted from at least 5 yards behind the line of scrimmage; the Spartans argued, to no avail, that Nagurski was closer to the line than that. Two years later, forward passing was legalized from any point behind the line of scrimmage.

from sideline to sideline and signifies the spot to which a team needs to advance the ball for a first down. Players and coaches don't see it, either. It's strictly a computer-generated line designed to enhance the viewing experience.

Natural or Artificial?

When the Houston Astrodome first opened in 1965, a healthy layer of natural turf covered its surface. But after just a few months of baseball season, it became apparent that grass could not survive for any length of time in an indoor stadium. An alternative was necessary, which hastened the development of a synthetic surface that came to be called

AstroTurf. And when the AFL's Houston Oilers moved into the Astrodome three years later, they became the first pro football team to play its home games on artificial turf. AstroTurf is a specific brand of synthetic turf originally developed by the Monsanto Company in the 1960s. The turf is placed over a protective pad that sits atop a base of asphalt. Only a few NFL teams have an AstroTurf field now. Most teams have gone back to natural grass. And several have a new synthetic turf—known as FieldTurf or other names depending on the manufacturer—that looks and feels almost like the real thing.

When artificial turf was new, even the bugs were fooled. In the 1960s the Philadelphia Eagles played their home games at Franklin Field on the University of Pennsylvania campus. The stadium's grass field was replaced by an artificial surface in 1969, but before the first game, the grounds crew had to clear the field of a big problem: thousands of dead grasshoppers who mistook the surface for the real thing!

Players had to get used to the fake stuff, too. As the Baltimore Colts Jim O'Brien lined up a potential game-winning field goal in the final seconds of Super Bowl V against the Cowboys, he reached down to pluck a few blades of grass to throw into the air and gauge the wind. But the grass wouldn't come up: Actually, the rookie kicker was so nervous that he didn't remember the game was being played on artificial turf. No matter, he made the kick and the Colts won 16–13.

I definitely preferred playing on grass to playing on carpet. I never played on the new stuff, though—FieldTurf. It does feel awfully

Moose's Memories

The Cowboys played the Houston Oilers in an American Bowl game in Mexico City one year (1994) right after the area had been drenched by a monsoon. And we just tore up the field, it was so wet and muddy. There were huge beetles in the grass. You'd be down in your stance waiting for the snap, and you'd see all these beetles crawling around down there by your hands and feet—nasty!

soft. Still, I don't think I would have liked it. It's an eye-phobia thing: I don't think I would have liked all those little black things that pop up when you run. It almost looks like dirt when you watch a game on television, but it's like little, chopped up pieces of old tires. That's a real big issue for me with my eyes, and I don't know how well I would have adjusted to it.

Most players say they run faster on the carpet, but I never really felt a difference between that and a good grass field. But soft turf did bother me. I hated soft turf. The last thing I needed was to be on a field that made me feel even slower than I really was!

Goalposts and Other Accessories

True to its roots in soccer and rugby, football rewarded kicking more than scoring touchdowns in its early days. In the early 1900s the current valuations of 3 points for a field goal and 6 points for a touchdown were set. But then as now, a field goal was recorded by kicking the ball through goalposts situated at either end of the field. The ball must carry through the goalpost's vertical uprights and over the horizontal crossbar.

The uprights of the goalpost line up with the hash marks on the field, which kickers can use to their advantage. Former NFL kicker Ray Wersching, for instance, never looked at the uprights when he trotted onto the field. Instead, he lined up his kick by looking at the hash marks. "The farther away you are, the narrower the goalposts look," he said. "But the hash marks always look wide."

The **goalposts** are held in place by a single standard, are painted bright gold, and are situated on each end line. The uprights are 18 feet, 6 inches apart and extend 30 feet above the crossbar, which is 10 feet off the ground. Ribbons are attached to the top of the uprights to help kickers gauge the strength and direction of the wind. For many years the posts were placed on the goal line, but in 1974 they were moved back to the end line to combat the growing proliferation of field goals.

History Book

The goalposts are painted bright gold because of a disputed kick in a 1965 NFL playoff game between the Green Bay Packers and the visiting Baltimore Colts. On a heavily overcast day, Green Bay's Don Chandler attempted a game-tying field goal in the fourth quarter that sailed very high past the left upright. Although the kick was ruled good, the Colts were furious because they believed it was wide of the mark. The next year, the uprights were extended and painted to help officials in their judgment.

Another aid to the officials are **pylons.** These small, orange markings stand at the corners of the end zone to highlight goal-line and end-line markings. The pylons are part of the end zone. So if you see a player striving for the goal line and he hits a pylon (or the ball hits it), it's a touchdown.

When it's too close for an official to determine if a play results in a first down, he calls in the **chain gang** for a measurement. From the sideline the men (or women) on the chain gang help track the exact spot on the field needed to make a first down. On every first down one member of the chain gang marks the spot with a brightly colored pole. That pole is connected to another by a chain 10 yards in length, which is stretched to its limit. This way, everybody knows where a team must advance the ball to begin a new set of downs. Another member of the chain gang holds a pole on the sideline that marks the start of each play. That pole also has a number atop it signifying the down.

Indoor and Outdoor Stadiums

From 1960 through 1981 the Minnesota Vikings enjoyed one of the NFL's most distinct home-field advantages when they played in the rigid climate of Metropolitan Stadium, where cold, snow, and ice often welcomed their opponents. Both the Vikings and their visitors had to play in the same weather, of course, but stoic Minnesota coach Bud Grant never would let his players acknowledge the cold. The Vikings had a psychological edge even before they took the field.

Then in 1982 Minnesota moved indoors to the newly built Hubert H. Humphrey Metrodome. But instead of relinquishing their home-field advantage, the Vikings enhanced it. Although the weather in the Metrodome was always a comfortable 72 degrees with no wind, opponents became unnerved by the deafening noise inside a stadium in which sound had nowhere to exit. The stadium quickly earned a nickname: "The Thunder Dome."

Soon other teams in cold-weather cities followed suit by moving into new, indoor stadiums. The proliferation of domes meant opposing players and coaches had to resort to hand signals and silent snap counts and pump in artificial noise to their own practices to prepare for the onslaught. Handling the sound "is as important as the plays—the Xs and Os," former NFL head coach Dan Reeves said.

Whether your favorite team plays most of its games indoors or outdoors could affect the philosophy employed by the coaches. The controlled climate and artificial turf indoors offer superior footing and cutting ability (that is, changing directions), and teams that play on it often place a premium on speed. Teams that play on natural grass, particularly those in more frigid climates, may be more inclined to place emphasis on other attributes. On the other hand, would a coach such as St. Louis's Mike Martz still call plays as aggressively outside as he does indoors? I think so. Would New England's Bill Belichick still employ his philosophy indoors? Probably.

Noise

When a team goes into an especially noisy place like the Metrodome, the critical thing for a player to do is to stay focused on the task at hand. Sometimes all the offensive linemen will hold hands, or the guard and the tackle will hold hands so the tackle doesn't have to look down at the center for the snap of the ball and take his eyes off the opposing player he is supposed to be blocking. The trouble with

History Book

The list of teams that play indoors doesn't include Dallas, which has played since 1971 in Texas Stadium, a facility that features a partial roof that keeps the fans covered but leaves the field open to the elements. Instead of making it a full dome, stadium plans allowed for a hole in the roof so, former Cowboys linebacker D. D. Lewis says, "God can watch his favorite team."

that, though, is it kind of tips off the other team that you're going to throw the ball.

There are other things you can do, too. You don't go on long counts so much—you snap the ball earlier more often. And the wide receivers need to look in and watch the snap of the ball to see when they can break from the line. Or players can go to a silent count, watching the quarterback for a signal to begin. Maybe he lifts his heel up. Then they start counting—"one one-thousand"—then the ball is snapped. But the offense has to be careful to mix that up now and then or it won't be long before the defense has figured it out, too. And if they do, the linemen will start teeing off on the quarterback.

Some teams, if they've got a road game in a dome or in an especially loud place like Kansas City, will try to practice with crowd noise, as mentioned before. Certain coaches just like to do that. They bring in speakers to practice and pump in crowd noise to simulate the experience you're going to have. Chan Gailey was the only coach I had with the Cowboys who did that. But I always felt it was a waste of time. You could never get it to the point that it was actually going to be during a game, and all it did was give me a headache.

Plus, I've never really bought into the crowd noise thing as a factor. I almost always could hear quarterback Troy Aikman. It was very rare that we were in a place and I couldn't hear him. Now I don't know if Emmitt Smith, who was lined up behind me, watched me or if he watched the players in front of us. Of course, I was directly behind the quarterback, so it's easy for me to say this, but if a player is focused on what he is doing, the noise should not be a deciding factor.

The Crowd

I never heard anything from the crowd when I was playing. That's a hard concept to explain to people. You know, how can you be in a place like the Rose Bowl—where the Cowboys played the Buffalo Bills in the Super Bowl one year—and not hear anything from 100,000 people? It's bizarre. But you're just so focused when you're on the field that you tune everything else out.

Now, of course, there are other times when you can't help but notice the fans. Like when you drive into the stadium on the team bus. You go into a place like Oakland, and they're just crazy. They're throwing things at the bus and everything else. I would just laugh at them.

There's nothing better than to go into a place like that and win— and drive them all out of there. Winning at home is great, but winning on the road at a difficult place to play—at Minnesota or Oakland or Philadelphia or Kansas City or old RFK in Washington—is just awesome.

My favorite place to play outside of Dallas was RFK Stadium in Washington (the Redskins played there until moving into FedEx Field in 1997). The Vet (Veterans Stadium in Philadelphia) was the worst. It was because of everything—the old carpet, the fans who hated us. They even booed Santa Claus there.

But I enjoy Philly now. My wife is from there, and it's one of my favorite cities to work as a broadcaster. I think the Eagles' organization is one of the best in the NFL, too. It's taken a while, but I think I am slowly becoming accepted by the fans there. They have great fans, who create a great home-field advantage. But without a doubt, I'd say the best fans are in Kansas City. The Chiefs have very intelligent, very football-savvy fans. You can't beat the sign on the Jumbotron that says, "Shhhhh! . . . Audible Zone."

CHAPTER FOUR

Equipment

Helmets

No high school, college, or professional football player would take the field today without the tools of his trade. These include the helmet and face mask, pads, and uniform. The helmet is the most distinctive—and important—piece of protective equipment for a player. It's a hard plastic shell that's custom-fit and lined with energy-absorbing internal materials that dissipate the force of an impact. Many models can be pumped with air or fluid while on the player's head, filling vinyl cushions for a more snug and secure fit. All helmets include a bar or cage called the face mask to protect the player's face.

Safety, of course, is always a big concern, and the NFL recently has been working with the people at NASCAR on concussion issues and helmets. You know, you see drivers who get in some pretty fierce crashes in those cars. Of course it's not practical to put a football player who has to do a whole bunch of running and changing directions into all that equipment that a stock-car racer has, but they're searching for ways to incorporate some of the plastic technologies into the helmets players wear now. Increased safety obviously benefits everybody.

For a long time—fifteen or twenty years, up until the last few years—helmets hadn't really changed much. Then one company came out with a lighter-weight helmet and that made some of the other helmet manufacturers take a look at what they were doing. So over the last three or four years, newer helmets have become lighter in weight but still provide the same or more protection against con-

Rules to Know

The helmet is intended solely as a protective device. NFL rules strictly prohibit using it as a weapon. Any player who butts, spears, or rams an opponent with his helmet costs his team a 15-yard penalty. More egregious offenses are subject to an ejection, fine, or suspension.

cussions, while at the same time improving ventilation and air circulation to help with heat-related problems.

Every player has to wear a helmet. It wasn't always that way of course. In the old days players didn't wear helmets. Or if they did, they were floppy leather ones that they could fold up and put in their pocket. I shudder to think what it would be like to be a lead blocker meeting one of today's hard-hitting linebackers square in the hole without wearing a helmet!

Helmets have been mandated since the early 1940s, although just about everyone was wearing one by then, anyway. The last man to go without a helmet is believed to be end Dick Plasman of the Chicago Bears, who played without a helmet in the 1940 NFL Championship Game. Pro Football Hall of Fame end Bill Hewitt, who played eight seasons for the Bears and Philadelphia Eagles before retiring in 1939, also refused to wear a helmet. But when he came out of retirement to play one more season in 1943, the league forced him to don one.

History Book

In 1948 Los Angeles Rams halfback Fred Gehrke, a former art student at the University of Utah, painted yellow horns on the team's helmets. It was the NFL's first helmet logo. When plastic helmets were approved one year later, it meant that color could be baked into them, and the widespread use of team logos and colors soon followed.

Face Masks

Players in the high-contact areas usually wear the most protective face masks. Offensive linemen, defensive linemen, linebackers, and fullbacks probably wear the largest face masks. The biggest decision for a player is whether to wear the bar that extends down the middle of the face. It can be distracting to your field of vision, but it takes only one fist to come through and make contact with your nose, or some fingers to inadvertently find their way into your eyes (there's that eye thing again!), to get you to adjust to having the bar.

Kickers and punters usually employ the smallest face masks because they are involved in the least contact. And, to ensure good visibility, quarterbacks rarely utilize the bar.

In the 1980s players began wearing face masks with tinted shields across the eyes. But players began wearing them solely to hide their eyes from the opposition, gaining a bit of an advantage. They eventually were prohibited unless a player had eye problems.

Communications

Head coaches long have been able to communicate via headsets with assistants watching the game from the press box upstairs. Between series, players (most often quarterbacks) have been able to grab a phone directly connected to those same coaches, who can see things from their vantage point that personnel on the field cannot. In the mid-1990s communication went a step further when coaches began talking to quarterbacks on the field via radio helmets.

Radio Helmets

As far back as the 1950s, Paul Brown, the innovative head coach of the Cleveland Browns, experimented with placing a radio receiver in his quarterback's helmet, but the device was banned by the NFL. The league tried its own experiment in the 1980s, but it failed. It tried again in the early 1990s, and by the 1996 regular season, the bugs had been worked out, and the head coach or one of his assistants began calling plays directly to the quarterback, instead of utilizing

History Book

Paul Brown's attempt at placing a radio receiver in quarterback George Ratterman's helmet in the 1950s ran into trouble during a preseason game in Chicago. At one point Ratterman stood in the huddle with a perplexed look on his face. "I'm getting cab calls from Michigan Avenue to State Avenue," he confided to his teammates.

hand signals or relying on players shuttling in and out of the lineup. Only the quarterback's helmet includes a radio receiver, and the quarterback can only hear the coach—he can't talk back. And though the quarterback receives the play from the sideline, he still can't expect any help with his on-field decision making. The electronic signal is cut off when the play clock reaches 15 seconds or the ball is snapped, whichever comes first.

The Uniform

Every team has two sets of uniforms, one with white jerseys and one with colored jerseys. It's up to the home team to decide which to wear: If the home team wears colored jerseys, the visiting team must wear white, and vice versa. Almost all teams choose to wear their colored jerseys at home, though it's not a requirement. The Cowboys, for instance, have had a long-standing tradition of wearing their white uniforms at home. After all, good guys wore white in the Old West. And besides it forced the opposition to wear dark uniforms in the heat early in the season.

Jerseys

Most jerseys today are made of a climate-friendly polyester mesh. But imagine playing a football game in canvas pants and a turtleneck sweater; that was the typical uniform in the late 1800s. Absurd as that may seem, those early uniforms gave way to another impractical idea:

Around the turn of the century, jerseys and pants were combined into one unit. The idea didn't last. Shortly after that, the first modern jerseys were manufactured from wool or cotton. Knits came along in the 1930s, and by the 1950s lighter synthetic jerseys made a breakthrough.

Numbers

Jersey numbers are taken for granted now, but it wasn't until the late 1930s that the NFL decreed that all players have numbers on the fronts and backs of their uniform. Today, numbers also appear on the jersey sleeves, with the player's last name embroidered across his back above the uniform number. Jersey insignias or team logos on the uniform date almost to the very beginning of American football. As far back as 1876, Princeton players wore a "P" on their football sweater.

One important thing to note when you're watching a game on television is that you can get a pretty good idea of what position a guy plays by the number on his jersey because there is a method to how the uniform numbers are doled out. (A version of this system was implemented by the NFL back in the 1950s; by the early 1970s the current system of numbering jerseys according to player position was fully adopted.) Numbers 1–19 generally are reserved for quarterbacks, kickers, and punters (though wide receivers also can wear numbers 11–19 now); 20–49 are for running backs and defensive backs (linebackers can wear 40–49 during the preseason, when rosters are larger than normal); 50–59 for centers and linebackers; 60–79 for guards, tackles, and defensive linemen; 80–89 for wide receivers and tight ends; and 90–99 for defensive linemen (linebackers also will sometimes wear 90–99).

I was a fullback—a running back whose primary responsibility is to block—so I wore number 48 in my career in Dallas.

Pants

Uniform pants today generally are manufactured from a knit incorporating spandex. That's a far cry from the original canvas pants that

History Book

One NFL team was named for the color of its jerseys. The Arizona Cardinals, a charter member of the league in 1920 while playing in Chicago, were originally formed in 1899 as a neighborhood team on that city's South Side. Two years later, founder Chris O'Brien bought some secondhand jerseys that were faded maroon in color. He called them "cardinal" red, and the name stuck. The Cleveland Browns, by the way, got their name from a local name-the-team contest in the 1940s—it was in honor of their coach, Paul Brown (though Brown didn't really like the idea of having the team named for him and floated the idea that perhaps fans suggested the name in honor of boxing champion Joe "The Brown Bomber" Louis).

were in vogue in the earliest days of football, when teams supplied jerseys and socks but players were left to rummage around for the rest of the uniform. Canvas pants couldn't have been very practical or comfortable, and they soon gave way to a variety of materials, primarily duck cloth, in the early 1900s. Synthetic fibers made inroads in the 1930s, and by 1934 the first knits appeared. Besides their composition the biggest change in football pants came in relation to padding. Early 1900s models of pants tried all sorts of complicated ways to tie or hold pads in place. Eventually, pants simply were made with pockets on the inside for thigh or knee pads.

Pads

Much like the evolution of the helmet, protective pads only grudgingly became accepted by football players in the early twentieth century, many of whom believed pads compromised the physical nature of the sport (read that to mean they believed it was more manly to play without them) or added too much bulk. But as players got bigger and the game got faster, pads quickly became an integral part of the uniform.

Shoulder Pads

The history of shoulder pads also mirrors the history of the helmet in that the first major breakthrough in protection came in the 1930s. Early leather shoulder pads gave way then to fiber shells that provided cantilevering, which held the pads high above the shoulders. The development gave football players their distinctive hulking appearance; more important, it absorbed much of the shock of an impact. Today's shoulder pads feature an air-impact system that makes them lighter and stronger than their predecessors, while distributing blows to a wider area. Players at different positions use different-size shoulder pads. The biggest pads are worn by linemen, the smallest by quarterbacks and kickers.

Perhaps no other sport has as wide an assortment of protective gear available to its players. The array of options includes thigh pads, knee pads, shin guards, elbow pads, forearm pads, hip pads, rib pads, neck rolls, bicep pads, and padded gloves. Any special pads, such as a flak jacket for a quarterback with injured ribs—air-filled tubes that work as shock absorbers—must be approved by the umpire before a game.

Shoes

Players wear different types of shoes depending on the surface and on field conditions. For instance, on artificial turf players don shoes with rubber nubs for better traction. On grass fields players wear cleats of interchangeable lengths to keep from slipping or sliding— longer cleats in rainy or muddy conditions or when the footing is not sure; shorter cleats on cleaner, faster tracks. Equipment men need to be ready at a moment's notice to change cleats during a game as the traction on the field becomes more or less slippery. They go right down the line of players and change the cleats in seconds—a lot faster than a player would do it—using an attachment on a cordless screwdriver.

The original football shoes simply were baseball shoes, often supplied by the players themselves, but innovations soon came along. Detachable cleats first were introduced in the 1920s. In the 1940s low-

History Book

The Sneakers Game

In 1934 the New York Giants defeated the Chicago Bears 30–13 in an NFL Championship Game that has come to be known as the "Sneakers Game." It was perhaps the most dramatic example of how the proper shoes can affect the outcome of a game.

The game was played in nine-degree temperatures in New York, and both teams donned their usual football cleats at the outset. But footing was treacherous on a field that was completely frozen, and Giants assistant equipment manager Abe Cohen was dispatched to nearby Manhattan College to borrow some rubber-soled basketball shoes. It was the third quarter by the time Cohen got back, and New York trailed 10–3. But the Giants changed their shoes and, buoyed by traction on the slippery turf, exploded to score 27 points in the fourth quarter and win 30–13.

Our Super Bowl win over the Buffalo Bills in January 1993 bears some similarity to the Sneakers Game. The game was played at the Rose Bowl in Pasadena, California, and as soon as the sun goes down in that stadium, the moisture on the field builds up and the turf gets real slippery. Well, that game kicked off in the sunshine, but it wasn't long before the sun went down behind the nearby mountains and shade crept across the field. Sure enough, players started slipping around, so when the offense came off the field, we went to the bench, and the equipment guys went right down the line changing us from ½-inch cleats to ¾-inch cleats. Then they did the same thing for the defense.

We were fortunate in that we had some players like quarterback Troy Aikman and safety James Washington who had played college football at UCLA, which used the Rose Bowl as its home field. Defensive end Charles Haley had joined us that year, too, and he was familiar with the soft turf on the West Coast from having played with the 49ers in Candlestick Park. So we had kind of a heads-up and made the change pretty quickly. The Bills never did change their cleats, and we won 52–17. I've had people tell me that changing our cleats played an important part in our victory.

cut shoes made their first appearance; by 1960 nearly everyone used them, and bulky, high-topped shoes became a quaint relic. In the 1970s teams adapted to the proliferation of artificial turf by donning footwear with short, hard-rubber cleats as part of the shoe.

Weather or Not

A football player is going to play in some poor-weather games, especially late in the season, so he might as well get used to it. And there are things he can do to combat the conditions. If he's playing on artificial turf, he might go to more studs on the bottom of his shoes. If he's on grass and it's a little wet or muddy or he feels like he needs a little extra grip, he might change to a ¾-inch cleat instead of a ½-inch cleat. Mostly, though, it's a matter of technique. He needs to remember to stay over his toes, keep his weight off his heels, and then be quick when he goes in and out of his breaks (changes direction).

In 1993 the Cowboys played the Miami Dolphins in Dallas on Thanksgiving Day in one of the worst games weatherwise I've ever played. It snowed that day. But not just a normal snow. It was snowing sleet balls. It was hard to throw the football down the field because when the receivers looked back to pick up the ball in the air, these little pellets came down on them. As soon as the receivers turned, they had to cover their eyes . . . which was great for me. Because we couldn't throw down the field, the ball had to be dropped off to the backs. I had eleven receptions—the highest number of catches in a game in my career.

Unfortunately, that game is mostly remembered for its bizarre ending. After we blocked a field-goal attempt late in the game, apparently to save a victory, Leon Lett, a defensive tackle, tried to pick up the ball and slipped, and the Dolphins recovered (a blocked field goal that goes beyond the line of scrimmage cannot be covered by the kicking team unless the defensive team touches it first). Given another chance, Miami kicked a field goal to win 16–14—but we never should have been in a position to lose that game in the first place.

The sideline is not a place to simply rest and recover. Players can view still photos of previous series if they were unsure about something they saw on the field.

Photo by Ron St. Angelo

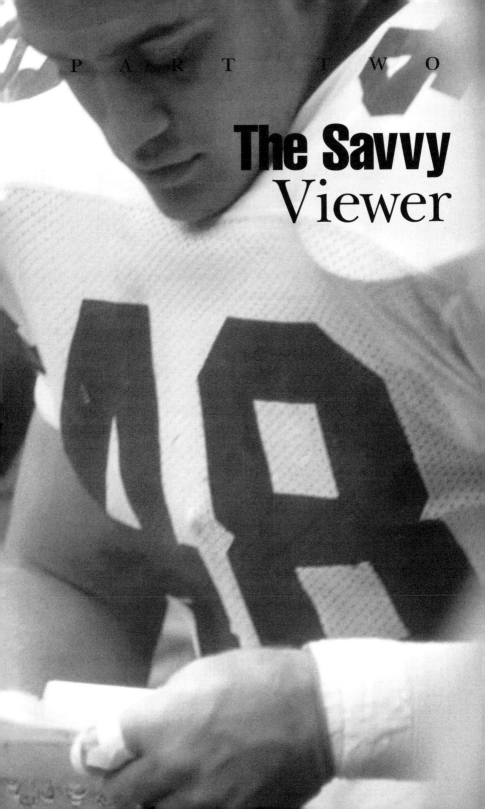

The Savvy
Viewer

My uniform these days is much different, but it is great to still be a part of the NFL and be close to the game.

Photo courtesy Fox Sports

A Player in the Booth

Made for Television

One of the big reasons football has become so popular in the United States is because it's the perfect game for television. The rectangular field fits nicely on the TV screen, and the starts and stops between plays naturally provide time for replay and analysis.

The marriage between football and television really began with the national telecast of the 1958 NFL Championship Game between the Baltimore Colts and the New York Giants. That game went into overtime and transfixed people all over the country. In fact, though it wasn't a particularly well-played game, the Colts' 23–17 victory was such an important landmark in football history in this country that it is commonly called the "Greatest Game Ever Played." Since then, television has helped carry the game into millions and millions of American households. NFL games, topped by the Super Bowl, which now is watched by more than 135 million people each year in 200 countries around the globe, consistently draw more viewers than most sporting events.

Experience Counts

A former player brings credibility to the broadcast booth that other broadcasters can't. Fans have become very intelligent about football, given all the information that is out there—radio, television, the Internet, and other media coverage that has become very meticulous. And even before the recent explosion in coverage over the Internet, John Madden revolutionized the way the games were done on television with insightful analysis that included his teaching and instruction about the game. Now there's twenty-four-hour sports talk radio, too.

There is just so much information out there that you have to be able to tell the fans just a little bit more to keep their interest. And that's where the former player comes in. "Tell me something different, something that I can't hear from all these other places, from all these people who didn't actually play the game," fans say.

That's where I come in. I've been there, so I know. But I also take my new role seriously. I played on offense, and I know that side of the ball real well. But now I have to familiarize myself with everyone—the defensive front seven, pass coverages, and personnel.

Back on the Field

The one thing television can't do is accurately present to the viewers the speed at which the game is played. I'm convinced that if people really could experience how fast the game is, they would be blown away. Sometimes even I lose the appreciation for that in the booth. So every game, I try to go down to the field beforehand and walk the field for a little bit. I make it a point to do that just to shock myself back into the feel for the game.

I like to go down to the field, too, if there's anybody down there I have a question for. I don't want to talk to everyone—whether coaches or players, they have a job to do, a game to prepare for. But sometimes I just have one question for a guy. And I don't want to bring him into a production meeting the day before the game and all of a sudden he is sitting there for fifteen or twenty minutes, so I'll just go down and see him during pregame warm-ups before they have their game faces on.

I also like to get down there to see what the conditions are like, and how the field is holding up. And just to watch the players, too, to try to get a feel for what the vibe is that day.

Thirty-Two Teams, One Goal

One of the perks of being a broadcaster is the exposure to all the different teams' philosophies and offensive and defensive schemes and game plans. It's wrong to think that you have all the answers. Sometimes you lose sight of the way organizations have different ways of approaching the same goal, which is winning games and winning a Super Bowl.

But I wouldn't say that we ever completely learn about the different philosophies for all thirty-two teams. It's a work in progress. Obviously, I know some teams better than others from doing more of their games—I work predominately with the NFC. So I feel that I know Philadelphia very well. Of course I know Dallas very well. I'm familiar with Chicago because their head coach, Lovie Smith, spent time in St. Louis, which I also know well due to Rams coach Mike Martz. I know the Falcons well because of head coach Jim Mora and offensive coordinator Greg Knapp and the time they spent in San Francisco. Ed Donatell is Atlanta's defensive coordinator. He came from Green Bay, another team I have covered quite often.

It is all about building trust. When you talk with a coaching staff and the players, they must trust you with any information they will give you. The more you are around them, the more of their trust you will earn.

For instance, on occasion we have been given information about specific plays. Mike Mularkey, who at the time was the offensive coordinator of the Pittsburgh Steelers, told us they were going to run a trick play within the first ten plays of the game. He gave us specific details to look for at the line of scrimmage before the play. The play was not successful, but we had earned his trust so that he gave us information about the game plan and didn't worry that we would reveal it. Once coaches and players trust you they become more specific and less evasive in their comments, which benefits our broadcast.

I can't imagine playing football in the "good ol' days." Does that helmet provide any protection? Thank goodness for technology.

Photo by Ron St. Angelo

CHAPTER SIX

A New Game

Not Like the Old Days

I think it's difficult for pro football fans today, at least for the adult fans. As kids they grew up rooting for one team. And they knew the players on that team generally were going to be the same from year to year; they knew if they devoted their allegiance to a star player, more than likely he was still going to be there the next season. But free agency has changed all that. Now players move from one team to another from year to year. That's one of the reasons fantasy football is so big—you can create your own team and follow those players, and it doesn't matter in what city they play.

It's not like college football, either. You devote your allegiance to your alma mater, and that doesn't change. You know the players are going to come and go every few years, but it's not as if they are going to go play for a competitor. How many stadiums are there on campuses now that hold 80, 90, or 100,000 people? College football is immensely popular.

People talk about the game not being played as well as it was in the past, and I think there's some validity to that. And the reason is free agency. That's not to say that today's athlete is not as good as in the past. To the contrary the potential of the contemporary athlete is greater every year. So I don't buy the argument that the talent in the NFL is diluted by having thirty-two teams. It's not watered down at all. When I came into the league in 1989, there were only twenty-eight teams. You can't tell me there wasn't enough talent out there to fill four more teams.

But it's very difficult to build team chemistry when players are coming and going year after year, and I think team chemistry is more important in football than in almost any other sport. You rely so much in football on what the other ten players around you on the field are doing on any given play.

To an extent a pitcher in baseball does that, but even a pitcher starts with the ball in his hands. He can strike out the side. Or a batter can hit a home run without the help of anyone else on his team. In basketball one superstar can make a difference. But in football, if you don't have eleven players working together, the play is not going to work. A quarterback needs to have the linemen up front protecting him and a wide receiver catching the ball. A running back needs to have the blocker to create space in which he can run. Even a kicker has to rely on the snapper and the holder to get a field-goal try off, as well as on the offensive line to keep the defense from blocking the kick.

Chemistry

In football each player has a job to do, and chemistry is so important. You know, there was a quite a stir with that lead-in to a 2004 Monday night game featuring Terrell Owens and an actress from *Desperate Housewives*. It wasn't the first time that Owens had been in the center of controversy—there was the time when he was playing for the 49ers that he pulled a pen out of his uniform sock and autographed a football immediately after scoring a touchdown.

That's all part of the "look at me"–type player, something that bothers me about today's NFL. Football is the ultimate team sport. It's the one sport where you really have to check your ego at the door—you are handing over a lot of control to other people.

In the era of free agency, and with salary-cap considerations, it's harder and harder to build the chemistry that is important to a football team. If you gave a big chunk of money to a couple of star players and you have to keep bringing new people to surround them every single year, there just aren't enough players who are around long enough to build that chemistry on a club.

That's why the New England Patriots are so remarkable. Coach Bill Belichick and Scott Pioli, New England's general manager, go get someone because of the type of player he is and how he will fit in with the team, not just because of his talent. They want a player who is a great teammate and loves to play football.

Another team that's following this same approach is Baltimore. Their general manager, Ozzie Newsome, has done a tremendous job of finding young players who are right for their system and bringing them in, especially through the draft. Only two first-round picks in the history of the Ravens (which officially began in 1996) are no longer on the roster, and both of those players—cornerback Duane Starks and wide receiver Travis Taylor—left via free agency. Even drafting low in the first round, they've found some great people: Ray Lewis with the twenty-sixth pick in 1996, Todd Heap with the thirty-first choice in 2001, and Ed Reed with the twenty-fourth selection in 2002.

Moose's Memories

We had remarkable team chemistry in my years in Dallas. By our third year or so there, running back Emmitt Smith and I knew what was expected of each of us, and each of us knew what the other was going to do on the field. This came not only from having played in the same backfield together, but also from having sat in so many meetings and everything else together. I can watch tapes of the Cowboys from the '90s now and see Troy Aikman and Jay Novacek and Emmitt and others all working together—we really had developed a chemistry. But you know, it took a long time to get there. And there just doesn't seem to be enough time to get to that point anymore.

Our Dallas teams had great chemistry during our Super Bowl run. I feel that gave us an advantage. Our confidence showed when we took the field.

Eight (Divisions) Is Enough

I think thirty-two teams—eight divisions with four teams each—is just perfect right now in the NFL. I know the league is always talking about needing a team in Los Angeles, since it is the number two television market, but unless it's a team that relocates, like a Minnesota or a New Orleans, I just don't think it's a good idea. You can't add just one expansion team because then you have an odd number at thirty-three. So then you have to get to thirty-four.

Besides, in LA they really get behind their college teams, USC and UCLA. I'm not sure that in a city with so many transplanted people, they'd really get behind a pro team. There's just too many other things to do in LA, too. In my opinion Los Angeles is different. It's just a totally different lifestyle.

Two great quarterbacks (Troy Aikman, left, and Terry Bradshaw) share a moment during pregame. Respect and camaraderie exist between all men who have played in the NFL.

Photo by Ron St. Angelo

Talking the Talk

Football Lingo

A lot of times we take it for granted on a telecast that the viewer knows exactly what we mean when we throw out various football terms. And chances are, if you're a big enough fan to tune in, you probably know what we're talking about when we say that the quarterback dropped back in the "pocket" or a team ran the ball to the "strong side."

But just in case you are new to the game, or just aren't familiar with some of its terms, here are some of the common words and phrases you are likely to hear whenever you are watching football—and which you may encounter throughout this book.

Audible. When the quarterback changes the play at the line of scrimmage, he is calling an audible. Sometimes he gets to the line and doesn't believe the play that was called will work against the defensive alignment—or he knows that another play *will* work against a particular defensive alignment—so he makes a change.

Backfield. The quarterback and his running backs compose the offensive backfield (the term also applies to the area in which these players line up). Sometimes the defensive backs are collectively referred to as the secondary, or the "defensive backfield."

Blitz. When there are more than four players rushing the quarterback, it's called a blitz. Sometimes, designated linebackers or defensive backs join the front four (or three, depending on the base defense) linemen in the pass rush.

Bump-and-run. The bump-and-run is a defensive technique utilized primarily by cornerbacks when they align themselves directly opposite, and close to, a wide receiver. The cornerback will bump the offensive player as he comes off the line of scrimmage (it's only allowed within the first 5 yards) to knock him off his route or disrupt his timing, then turn and run with him in man-for-man coverage.

Coin toss. Before the teams take the field for the start of the game, the referee meets with captains from both sides and tosses a coin. The winner of the coin toss has the option of choosing either to receive the ball or defend a particlar end of the field. Most teams choose to receive the ball, but in some instances—particularly when wind or other adverse weather conditions are a factor—defending a particular end of the field may be more important. This is especially true in the second half, when the team that lost the coin toss gets its choice and may want to be assured of going in a particular direction in the fourth quarter, when a close game could be decided. In college football the team that wins the coin toss can defer its choice to the second half, giving its opponent the choice at the beginning of the game, but teams cannot do that in the NFL.

Flat. A quarterback will often dump off a short pass to the running back in the "flat." It's the general area that runs 3 to 5 yards beyond the line of scrimmage from the player at the end of the line of scrim-mage to the sideline.

Hang time. Hang time—the length of time that a punt stays in the air—is measured from the time the ball leaves the punter's foot to the time it is caught or hits the ground. It's important because it gives the punter's teammates time to race downfield and cover the kick.

"I" formation. When the two running backs line up directly behind the quarterback (forming an "I"), they are in an I formation. In Dallas I often lined up behind quarterback Troy Aikman to lead block for running back Emmitt Smith, who was positioned directly behind me. An offset I would have the fullback lined up splitting the inside leg of the tackle (either strong side—the side on which the tight end lines up—or weak side, depending on the play call in the huddle).

Illegal motion. Only one offensive player is allowed in motion (see "man in motion") before the snap. If two players are in motion at the same time, the offensive team is penalized (unless the players come to a reset and are still for one full second prior to the snap).

Line of scrimmage. The line of scrimmage is imaginary and extends from sideline to sideline at the spot of the ball. The offense must have seven players on the line of scrimmage for every play. Defensive players can line up anywhere on their side of the line of scrimmage.

Man in motion. When a tight end, receiver, or running back goes in motion, he runs behind, and parallel to, the line of scrimmage. Only one man is allowed in motion at any given point before the snap; he is not allowed to move forward until the play starts.

Man-for-man coverage. In pass defense each eligible receiver has a linebacker or defensive back who is assigned specifically to cover him. The defender will stay with his man wherever he goes on the field.

Muff. A muff occurs when a player touches a free ball but never actually has possession of it. The distinction is important because of the rules for advancing a free ball. On punts, for instance, if the return man touches the ball while trying to make a catch but never physically has possession—a muff—the kicking team is allowed to recover the ball but cannot advance it.

Neutral zone. The neutral zone is similar to the line of scrimmage. This is an area equal to the width of the football that extends along the line of scrimmage and upon which the defense cannot infringe prior to the snap.

Onside kick. An onside kick is a specific type of kick that the kicking team attempts to cover. You'll most often see it after a team scores late in the game but still trails, but it can be an effective surprise play at other times. By rule the kicking team can cover any kickoff, but the onside kick is the only viable opportunity—the ball needs to travel only 10 yards (unless touched by a player on the receiving team before traveling 10 yards).

Option pass. When a running back takes a handoff as if on a normal run but pulls up and throws the ball downfield (the running back must still be behind the line of scrimmage when making the throw), he is throwing an option pass. The player attempting to throw is protected under all the rules that are afforded the normal quarterback.

Pass interference. When a defensive player illegally obstructs an offensive player's opportunity to catch a pass, it is called pass interference. There are several classes of pass interference, which are explored in the next chapter.

Play-action pass. A play-action pass begins with a fake handoff to a running back. A good play-action quarterback, creating the illusion of a running play, can freeze a defense's pass rush and get the linebackers to step up and create separation for his receivers. He also buys himself extra time to look for pass catchers downfield.

Play clock. Teams have 40 seconds from the end of one play to begin the next. A play clock operates independent of the game clock and tracks the time left before the ball must be snapped. Quarterbacks keep a wary eye on the play clock, lest their team incur a 5-yard penalty for delay of game if it expires before they get off a play.

Pocket. The pocket is the area that the quarterback's blockers have created to protect him. It's in the part of the field between the offensive tackles and behind the line of scrimmage.

Red zone. It's not red, and it's not even marked, but players, coaches, and fans are acutely aware of the red zone: the area on each side of the field from the goal line to the 20 yard line. The league's top teams usually are the ones who play best—offensively and defensively—in the red zone. On offense scoring opportunities are too precious to be wasted. On defense a stop inside the red zone can give a team a big lift.

Sack. A defensive player who tackles the quarterback before he can get off a pass play is credited with a sack. (The term was coined by Pro Football Hall of Fame defensive end Deacon Jones, a member of the Rams' "Fearsome Foursome" defensive line in the 1960s and 1970s, who made it his specialty.)

Scheme. A devised plan of attack that an offense or defense utilizes. A defense could use a zone blitz scheme. An offense may want to expand on their vertical passing scheme.

Seam. A seam is an area in between defenders in zone coverage.

Secondary. The cornerbacks and safeties make up the defense's secondary. The term can also apply to the area of the field in which the defensive backs usually align.

Snap. The snap is the exchange of the ball from the center that sets each play in motion.

Strong side. The side of the offensive line on which the tight end lines up at the beginning of a play is called the strong side. If the tight end moves in motion, an offense can change its strength to gain an advantage over the defense.

Three-point stance. When a player lines up with one hand on the ground, he's in a three-point stance (the three "points" being the two feet and the hand; if both hands are on the ground, it's called a four-point stance).

Time-out. Each team is allowed to stop the clock with a time-out as many as three times in each half (and twice in an overtime period). Sometimes a time-out is utilized to discuss strategy, other times merely to preserve time on the clock.

Touchback. A touchback occurs when a ball is whistled dead behind a team's end-zone line. For instance a punt or kickoff that the receiving team does not return out of its own end zone is ruled a touchback. So, too, for a pass that a defensive team intercepts in the end zone and does not choose to return. On all touchbacks the ball is placed at the 20 yard line.

Two-minute warning. The two-minute warning is official notification to each team that two minutes remain in the first half or in the game. If a play is under way when the clock reaches two minutes, notification comes when the play stops.

Weak side. The side of the offensive line that does not have a tight end on it is called the weak side.

Zone coverage. As opposed to man-for-man coverage, in which each defender is assigned an offensive player, the cornerbacks and safeties (and linebackers) in zone pass coverage are assigned a specific area of the field for which to be responsible.

Referee Ed Hochuli signals that a touchdown has been scored.

Photo courtesy of Ed Hochuli

CHAPTER EIGHT

Officials and Penalties

Men in Stripes

Every sport has its on-field arbiters, and in football it's up to a team of seven officials to enforce the rules, assess penalties, and spot the ball. Each official has a whistle he can blow to stop play and a yellow penalty flag he throws to indicate an infraction. NFL officials are easy to spot: They wear black-and-white striped shirts.

Instant Replay

If you've ever tuned into an NFL game and seen the referee under a black drape and peering into a box, looking like some nineteenth-century photographer, you've seen instant replay at work.

Instant replay long has existed as an enhancement to television broadcasts, but in 1978 the NFL began experimenting with the use of instant replay as a tool to aid officials. After various incarnations, none of which garnered lasting support among owners and coaches, the NFL adopted its current version of instant replay in 1999, and it's proved to be popular with league personnel and fans. Previously, the decision was made in the replay booth by an official designated by the NFL. Now the referee on the field makes the final call.

Now, about that black drape. It covers a monitor on which the referee can view a challenged play from as many angles as the game's television coverage allows. He has 90 seconds to uphold or reverse the official's original decision, and he will reverse it only if the evidence is indisputable.

One thing about instant replay: It has proved that NFL officials are right most of the time.

"Down by Contact"

The one thing I think the NFL needs to do with instant replay is make "down by contact" reviewable. "Down by contact" refers to plays on which a ballcarrier apparently fumbles, but the official has blown a whistle to stop the play. It's not reviewable by instant replay, and that's just plain ridiculous. Look at the Dallas and Philadelphia Monday night game in 2004: The Cowboys recovered a fumble near the Eagles' 10 yard line in the first quarter, but the officials ruled the runner was down by contact when the ball was fumbled with him standing straight up. The Eagles went on to win pretty easily, but who knows how the game might have been different if the Cowboys got that ball and scored an early touchdown?

At the owners' meetings in March of 2005, they voted once again that "down by contact" is not reviewable. A proposal to change the policy needed twenty-four votes from the league's thirty-two owners, but it got only twenty.

In Search of Perfect Replay

Let me just say that I think the officials these days do a really good job. There is so much gray area—both on the calls and on the replays—that it makes it tough on them, and they do a fabulous job.

There's never going to be a perfect replay system. As long as you have replay, you're never going to have officials just making calls and not worrying about the ramifications. It's human nature for people not to be as sure of themselves when they know they are going to get second-guessed. You just can't have it both ways. Some have suggested having separate crews on the field and in the booth so the field officials don't look bad. Pace of play is always an issue, but I don't think it affects replay. I think what frustrates fans, whether they are in the stadium or watching at home, is that even after viewing the replay, they disagree with the official's ruling. I said it before: The officials do a great job. However, as they try to make the rules more black and white, I think they create more shades of gray. There are too many "if, then" scenarios.

It's like a coach striving for that absolutely perfect offensive or defensive scheme. It's just not there. But as long as you keep the gray area shrinking and the black-and-white area growing, then I think you're headed in the right direction.

Replay Challenges

Under the replay challenge system, each team is allowed to challenge an official's decision up to twice per game (other than during the final two minutes of each half). But a challenge can be costly: The team is charged with a time-out, which is restored if the challenge is successful but lost if it is not. A team that does not have any time-outs left cannot make a challenge. However, in the final two minutes of each half and in overtime, a replay assistant in a booth in the press box can initiate as many reviews as necessary. (A team that wins both challenges gets a third as long as it still has a time-out at its disposal.)

Only certain types of plays can be challenged, such as whether a player had possession of the ball in the end zone or if a pass was complete or incomplete or intercepted. Judgment calls, such as whether a defender interfered with a pass receiver, cannot be challenged.

Managing Replay Challenges

A coach can't save his challenges and hope they are there for him later in a game. He needs to use them when he needs them. He can't let one go by figuring that he may want to save it for the fourth

Moose's Memories

As a player I hated all the stoppages in a game—the replay delays, the television time-outs. The worst was standing around in the huddle on a change of possession, when you are anxious to get out of the commercials and get a drive started. At that point the offense has already had a breather when the defense was on the field; now the players are just anxious to get going. Now that I'm on the other side, though, I have a little more sympathy for the television networks!

quarter because who knows what the situation is going to be by then? It won't do him any good if he's down by 17 points but still has two replay challenges left. Rams coach Mike Martz has received a lot of criticism for his use of challenges, but it is a coach's discretion what he considers a momentum-changing play.

It's like managing for Game 7 of the World Series. You've got to worry first about winning Game 6.

The Referee

While each official has his own duties and jurisdiction, it's the referee who has the ultimate authority and control of the game. He's the most visible official because he's the one who signals all penalties to the team benches, fans, media, and television audience. The referee also is the only one who wears a white cap. The rest of the officials wear black caps.

Other Officials

On a play from scrimmage, the referee lines up 10 to 12 yards in the offensive backfield, while the umpire is across the line of scrimmage 4 or 5 yards on the defensive side of the ball. The head linesman and line judge straddle the line of the scrimmage near opposite sidelines at the start of a play, while the field judge, side judge, and back judge take positions down the field. Because they're in the middle of all the action, the officials need to be well conditioned and quick on their feet.

If you want to know where the ball will be spotted for the next play (or if a ballcarrier has made the requisite yardage for a first down or scored a touchdown), watch the head linesman and the line judge as they race from the sidelines toward the hash marks at the conclusion of a play. The referee takes his cue from those officials, who help him determine where forward progress was stopped.

Penalties

Penalties create a lot of hidden yardage that isn't accounted for in the game stats. You always hear about a team's total yards gained or total yards allowed in a game—that's net yards rushing plus net yards passing (passing yards minus yards lost on sacks). It's on the total yards category that the NFL ranks its offensive and defensive leaders for the season. But what you don't often hear about is the yardage gained or lost via penalties. And it's not just the actual yardage of the penalty: 5, 10, or 15 yards. If an offense has an 18-yard gain that is wiped out by a 10-yard penalty, to me that's 28 yards of effective field position that it has just lost.

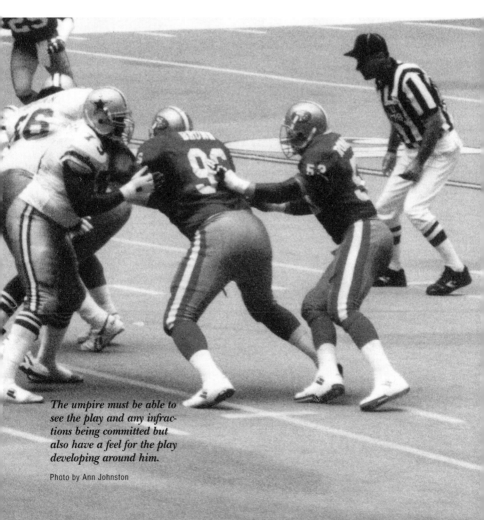

The umpire must be able to see the play and any infractions being committed but also have a feel for the play developing around him.

Photo by Ann Johnston

A Referee's Signals

Referees utilize a series of hand signals to communicate the nature of a penalty, touchdowns, first downs, or other on-field happenings. If it's a penalty, he'll signal which team it's against by pointing to the end of the field it's defending (today's officials also are equipped with wireless microphones to voice the infraction and offer any accompanying details, such as the number of the offending player). Here are some of the most common referee's signals you see while watching a game.

Touchdown:
Both arms extend above head.

First down:
Arm points in the direction in which the offensive team is moving.

Time-out:
Hands crisscross above head.

Delay of game:
Arms fold in front of chest.

Illegal motion:
One hand moves in a horizontal arc.

Personal foul *(such as hitting the quarterback after the ball has been released, grabbing and holding onto a player's face mask, or other unnecessarily rough acts):* One wrist strikes the other above head.

Holding: One hand grasps the opposite wrist, fist clenched, in front of chest.

Incomplete pass: Arms crisscross in front of the body.

Pass interference: Open hands extend forward as if pushing something.

Offside *(when the defense encroaches across the line of scrimmage before the snap or into the neutral zone between the offensive and defensive lines):* Hands on hips.

False start *(such as when a player on the offensive team begins moving before the ball is snapped):* Forearms rotate in front of body.

Referee's signals courtesy of the NFL

Intentional Grounding and Pass Interference

Two of the more controversial (and most difficult to understand) penalties are intentional grounding and pass interference.

Intentional Grounding

The penalty on the offense for intentional grounding is steep: 10 yards and a loss of down—most penalties do not incur a loss of down charge, and the team against whom the infraction was committed has the option of accepting or declining. Intentional grounding is called on a quarterback (or anyone throwing the ball) who, to avoid being tackled for a loss by a pass rusher, purposely throws a pass "without a realistic chance of completion." Obviously, that's a little open-ended. As long as an eligible receiver is in the area of the pass, a quarterback will not be called for intentional grounding. And a couple of seasons ago, the rule was altered in an effort to protect a scrambling quarterback. Any quarterback who has scrambled out of the pocket but is still behind the line of scrimmage can throw the ball away as long as he throws it beyond the line of scrimmage.

Pass Interference

Pass interference is another tough one because it's never really clearcut. The rule says that no player may "significantly hinder the progress of an eligible player of such player's opportunity to catch the ball."

Either an offensive or defensive player can be called for pass interference, though the majority of the time it is called on the defense. The penalty for offensive pass interference is 10 yards back from the previous spot of the ball. The penalty on the defense is an automatic first down at the spot of the foul. If the interference occurs in the end zone, it's an automatic first down, and the ball is placed at the defending team's 1 yard line.

Rules to Know

There are six classes of pass interference:

1. Contact without playing the ball

2. Playing through the back of the wide receiver

3. Grabbing the wide receiver's arm

4. The "arm bar" (when a defender runs down the field side by side with the receiver and uses his arm to prevent the receiver from a chance at catching the ball)

5. Cutting off the path of the receiver without playing the ball

6. "Hook and turn" (hooking the receiver and turning his body prior to the arrival of the ball)

The key thing to remember is that both the offensive and defensive players have a right to the ball. Contact incidental to either player's ability to catch the ball is not called interference, and officials also are instructed not to call interference if there's any question whether contact is incidental or not. The important thing for the defender to do is to get his head back around to pick up the flight of the ball. It's when the defender makes contact and doesn't get his head turned around that he's sure to be whistled for pass interference.

We didn't try to trick anybody with our offensive approach in Dallas; we challenged teams to stop us. That approach led to three Super Bowls, the first in Pasadena against the Buffalo Bills.

Photo by Ron St. Angelo

PART THREE

Offense

For a play to be successful, every player has to do his job. No wonder Emmitt Smith became the NFL's all-time leading rusher—even I could gain 6 yards with that blocking.

Photo by Ann Johnston

CHAPTER NINE

The Play Call

Coach's Choice

The days of 3 yards and a cloud of dust are long gone in football. (You can't have a cloud of dust on a FieldTurf surface, anyway—3 yards and a "cloud of crushed rubber"?) Many teams routinely pass more than they run, a concept unheard of even just twenty-five or thirty years ago. And many offensive philosophies, such as what is known as the West Coast Offense, now utilize a short passing game to help set up the run—it always used to be the run that set up the pass—or to maintain ball control.

Almost all plays are called by the coaches. The offensive coordinator relays the play to the quarterback through a receiver in the player's specially equipped helmet. That's why sometimes you'll see the quarterback standing outside of the huddle with his hands over the ear holes in his helmet, trying to concentrate on the play being called. Sometimes a head coach is the play caller, such as Mike Holmgren in Seattle or Jon Gruden in Tampa Bay.

Not even the Colts Peyton Manning, who probably has more flexibility than most quarterbacks, calls his own plays nowadays. Sometimes Peyton will come to the line of scrimmage with different plays to choose from, then he picks the one he thinks will be the most successful. He might have left the huddle with the formation called, then he decides whether it's going to be a running play or a passing play depending on what he sees in presnap. Even in this Peyton is the exception, though. Generally, it's the coaches who call the plays.

History Book

It used to be that quarterbacks called all of their own plays, and you can still find an old-timer now and then who bristles at the thought of someone on the sidelines making those decisions. Those guys felt like it was part of the quarterback's job to call the plays, and they believed that a quarterback had a better feel for what was happening on the field. The philosophy now is that a quarterback has enough to worry about with today's sophisticated offenses and coverage schemes without the added responsibility of play calling, too.

The man who was most responsible for that shift was Paul Brown. He coached the Cleveland Browns in the old All-America Football Conference in the late 1940s, and then when they joined the NFL beginning in 1950. Brown had one of the all-time great quarterbacks on his team, Otto Graham, but he still believed in calling the plays himself. He utilized an innovative method of shuffling the Browns guards in and out of the lineup as messengers. Graham hated the idea. He wanted to call his own plays, just like every other quarterback in the league at the time. But it was hard to argue with the results: From 1946 to 1955 the Browns played in ten consecutive league title games (four in the AAFC and six in the NFL), and they won seven of them.

Audibles

How much a quarterback audibles, or changes the play at the line of scrimmage, really is an individual matter. Someone like the Indianapolis Colts Peyton Manning is going to be given more leeway than even, say, the Philadelphia Eagles Donovan McNabb. And McNabb obviously is going to be given more leeway than a young quarterback such as the New York Giants Eli Manning or the Pittsburgh Steelers Ben Roethlisberger. It all depends on a team's offensive system, on a quarterback's relationship with his offensive coordinator, and on how much responsibility the quarterback can handle.

As noted before, Peyton Manning is very unusual in the flexibility he is allowed to change plays at the line of scrimmage. I think that maybe the confidence that the Colts have in him is unprecedented. It's a combination of the system being employed and the trust that Indianapolis offensive coordinator Tom Moore has in Peyton's ability to execute that system. You know, a lot of people used to kid Terry Bradshaw—the great Pittsburgh Steelers quarterback of the 1970s and now a studio analyst for NFL games on television—that, sure, he called his own plays, but he only had six plays to call! But Peyton Manning can go to the line with that many plays to choose from at one time, then opt for the one that he thinks will work best. So a lot of it just has to do with the individual.

A quarterback who changes the play at the line of scrimmage will call out a live code word to alert his teammates to the audible. It could be a color or a number and could change from time to time during the season. The quarterback also can call out a code word that isn't live (a dummy audible) to throw off the defense.

Rules to Know

While modern technology has made it possible for offensive coordinators to radio plays to the quarterback, it also puts the quarterback under pressure to assimilate the call, relay it to his teammates in the huddle, get up to the line of scrimmage and get his team set, and get the ball snapped—all in time before being assessed a delay of game penalty.

The rule is that an offensive team has 40 seconds in which to get off a play. As soon as one play ends, the play clock begins counting down from 40 until the next snap. After certain stoppages, such as time-outs or penalties, the play clock begins at 25 seconds on the referee's whistle.

Sometimes you might notice the referee pump one arm vertically into the air. He's telling the operator to reset the play clock to 25 seconds. If the referee pumps both arms into the air, he's telling the operator to reset the clock to 40 seconds.

Passing Plays

Here's a typical play call from my days in Dallas: "I Right, Scat Right, 5-2-5 F Post. On Two."

"I Right" is the formation, which is the typical I formation with the strong side, or where the tight end lines up, on the right. "Scat Right" is the protection, with "scat" meaning a free release for the fullback (because he has no pass protection responsibility, he can go directly to his route), leaving six men in to block, with the tailback blocking on the weak side.

"5-2-5" means the two wide receivers run 5 routes (see the Passing Tree diagram on page 67), which are 18-yard comebacks to the outside, while the tight end (the second number called) runs a 2 route, which for him is a little drag route toward the middle. "F Post" means the fullback runs a post route. And finally, "On Two" is the count on which the ball is snapped, usually at the sound of "hut" by the quarterback.

You can see how things would change on other play calls. The routes might be "7-8-7," where the two wide receivers run 7 routes (see the Passing Tree diagram) to the corner and the tight end runs an 8 to the post, or "9-8-9," where the outside guys run go routes.

Gridiron Glossary

X-Y-Z

The route numbers in a passing play are in **X-Y-Z** order with **X** usually being the split end (the wide receiver split wide on the line of scrimmage), **Y** being the tight end, and **Z** being the flanker (the wide receiver lined up on the tight-end side, but off the line of scrimmage).

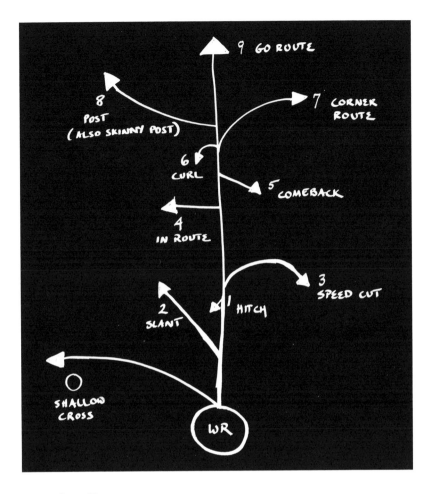

Passing Tree

Every team has some version of a passing tree. For the Cowboys receivers it was a straight line up the field with different numbers representing the depths and directions of the routes the players would take at the snap. A "0" route was a shallow drag, almost coming off the line of scrimmage. A "1" was a hitch, straight up the stem 5 yards, then turn around and come back a bit. A "2" was a slant, a couple of steps off the line of scrimmage, then a break to the middle. The "3" was a speed cut out to the side, the "4" an in route about 12 yards, the "5" an 18-yard comeback, the "6" a deep curl, the "7" toward a corner, the "8" a post, and the "9" a go route.

You see the same routes pretty much everywhere. It's just that different systems use different combinations. In the West Coast Offense, for instance, they like to construct triangles. So they might have a curl, a flat, and a tight end over the top of the ball, creating kind of a triangle of pass catchers for the quarterback to choose from. Other systems use tiers, in which one receiver runs an intermediate route, another runs a shallow route, and a third runs a deep route.

The term "West Coast Offense" has come to be stamped on a wide range of offenses, but all are characterized by a ball-control system predicated on short, high-percentage passes. Though the roots of the West Coast Offense go back before Bill Walsh, the 49ers head coach, it was he who popularized it in San Francisco in the 1980s.

In Dallas the running backs' routes were called by word and always tagged on the end of the receivers' routes, as in "5-2-5 F Post" in the above example or "9-4-0 F Corner" or "9-8-9 Backs Cross," with "F" being the fullback. But if we broke formation and I was in the slot or split wide, then I had to know if I was the single receiver and had the first number, or if I was the split end with the third route.

Moose's Memories

A few times, you'd break the huddle and just forget what the play call was. The first time I ever played in the Super Bowl was in the 1992 season (Super Bowl XXVII, in which the Cowboys routed Buffalo 52–17). We had a Friday practice before the game when we went over the scripted plays—the first several plays of the game. We called the first play, and it took me three times to get it. We broke the huddle and I said, "Check!" Troy Aikman wanted to know what was wrong. I said, "I don't know what to do." So we got back in the huddle, they called the same play again, and this time we got about two steps farther before I said, "Check!" again. "Are you kidding me?" Troy said. I said, "I'm just going blank here." By the third time I got it right.

Gridiron Glossary

"In the Slot" or "Split Wide"?

The offense will displace running backs and fullbacks in the formation to try to create mismatches in the passing game or to disguise plays to confuse the defense. For instance the Eagles will try to isolate Brian Westbrook (number 36) in passing situations versus a safety or linebacker by displacing him in the formation.

The other reason to displace the backs is to indicate a formation that shows a strong pass tendency to get the defense in a certain alignment and then run the ball. They are trying to get favorable blocking schemes.

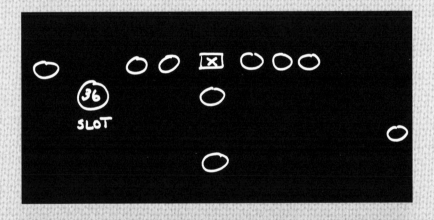

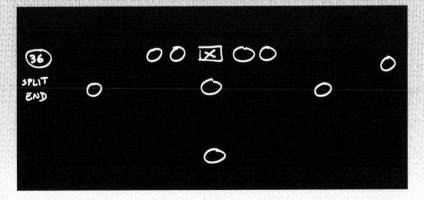

Running Plays

In Dallas we called our passing plays by numbers and our running plays by words. A lot of teams do it the other way around, with running plays by numbers and passing plays by words, but I always thought that could get a little verbose with all the different possibilities. To me the Cowboys' system was very user friendly. Still, even if the terminology is different, everyone utilizes the same basic running plays.

For teams that use numbers, the first number in a play call refers to the running back and the second number to the hole in which the play is designed to go. Odd numbers generally are to the left side of the line and even numbers to the right. So "I Right 22" means an I formation, with the strong side (the tight-end side) on the right, the number two back taking it to the number two hole, which would be between guard and tackle.

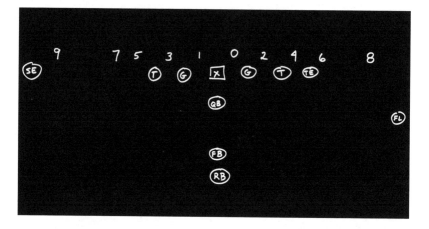

With the Cowboys, since we didn't use numbers, we called plays such as "lead draw left" or "lead draw right" or "press right." Everyone has those plays; everyone has a strong-side lead or a press play.

A press play is most noticeable when watching a team like Indianapolis, where Peyton Manning really stretches to get the ball to Edgerrin James and the linemen run shoulder to shoulder. Edgerrin might start running the ball to the left, but then he can go anywhere the hole is. By the way, all running plays are designed to go to a specific area, but the running back has the freedom to take the ball to the open hole along the line of scrimmage. Defensive players also have a job to do, so the play doesn't always work as it was designed.

The big rule on the press play is that you can't cut back anywhere behind your center. That doesn't necessarily mean where the center is in the blocking scheme, but where he was when the play started. If the play starts on the left hash mark, then the press play should never come back behind the left hash. Now Edgerrin might start out to the left and cut back all the way behind the right guard's block, but that might be 3 or 4 yards outside the hash. The Colts are just trying to get everybody moving and "press" the hole. If Edgerrin is running to the left, he can take it to the 1, 3, 5, or 7 hole—wherever he sees that the play might be the most successful.

The biggest difference among teams on running plays is in the blocking schemes. In Dallas, for instance, we usually utilized a man blocking scheme. Watch Kansas City play, and you'll see an example of a zone blocking scheme, one in which your linemen go shoulder to shoulder and just try to create a push on the defenders.

Gridiron Glossary

Levels

On the defense there are three levels. The first level is the defensive line, the second is the linebacker level, and the third is the secondary. If an offensive lineman is supposed to block a defensive lineman and he misses, he should go to the next level, which is the linebacker level. The fullback, whose responsibility would be the linebacker, would pick up the defensive lineman who was missed and basically switch assignments with the offensive lineman who missed his block.

In Dallas we leaned more toward everyone having an individual assignment. We were trying to create a hole, where in a scheme such as Kansas City's, they're trying to create a wall and get everybody running, then let the back decide where to take the ball.

If you are going to play in the Super Bowl, your quarterback has to play well. Number 8 with the ball, Troy Aikman's sole motivation was to be a champion.

Photo by Ron St. Angelo

CHAPTER TEN

The Quarterback

Two Sides Are Better Than One

Just like any other position on the football field, there are two sides
to playing quarterback: the physical side and the mental side. But
also just like everything else, those components are magnified when it
comes to playing quarterback because of the nature of the job. It's
the glamour position in football, and the quarterback is the most visible player on the field.

I've seen every kind of quarterback. There are the guys who are
blessed with all the physical tools—they can throw the ball on a rope
to a spot the size of a dime or scramble away from pressure and
throw on the run—but they don't understand the mental side of
things. Then there are those players who don't have a lot of the physical skills, but they understand the importance of the mental side of
the game.

You watch some of the quarterbacks who have the skills, like Jeff
George or Ryan Leaf, and you think they can't miss. You figure
they're going to be stars in the NFL for a long time. But they just
don't understand that physical tools alone aren't enough. Then there
are guys who seem to stick around forever who aren't nearly as physically talented. In Dallas we had Jason Garrett, who was a backup to
Troy Aikman for a long time, and I think of guys like Todd Philcox,
my quarterback at Syracuse who stayed in the NFL for several years.
There are some quarterbacks out there right now, such as Doug
Pederson and Koy Detmer, who may be career backups but they
understand what it takes to be successful and make up for their physical shortcomings with their preparation and professional approach.

History Book

Indianapolis Colts quarterback Peyton Manning had a season for the ages in 2004. He passed for 49 touchdowns to break Dan Marino's twenty-year-old NFL record by 1. Manning also passed for 4,557 yards and easily shattered the league's single-season record with a passer rating of 121.1. Peyton did it all in only fifteen games, too—he sat out almost all of the Colts' last regular-season game because his team already was locked into its spot in the playoffs.

Obviously, it's the quarterbacks who possess both the physical and mental skills who really stand apart from the rest. It's really special when you find someone who has both sides of the equation going for him. That's when you've got a Troy Aikman or a Peyton Manning or a Dan Marino. Those are the ones who are physically blessed with God-given ability, and they get the mental side, too. Then on top of it, they never lose sight of the work ethic that got them where they are.

"Managing" the Game

I find that the role of the quarterback has changed quite a bit over the past several years. A lot of coaches want quarterbacks to "manage" the game, instead of win it. When I was playing, the quarterback wasn't a manager, he was a game breaker. You wanted your quarterback to be the driving force of your team, a player who was good enough to win a game on his own if need be.

That "It" Factor

What truly separates the superstar quarterback from the rest of the pack is something that nobody has really been able to define. It's one of those intangibles that announcers and the media are always talking about. We kind of kid around and say they've got that "'thing,' you know, they've got 'it.'"

"It" is something like charisma. People want to follow the player who has "it." He comes into the huddle and—even as a young guy—he instantly has credibility with his teammates. You can try to explain that to people all day long and it won't do any good, but as soon as they meet him they instantly can see that he's got "it." "Yeah, now I see what you're talking about," they'll say. It's just a confidence that exudes from the player.

Here's a tip: If you want to know if a quarterback has "it," watch his eyes. If you're in the stands, you're not going to be able to, of course. But if you're watching on television, the camera shots get so close these days, you can see them. Watch the quarterback's eyes for a calm sense of purpose and resolve.

Washington's Patrick Ramsey is one of the young players in today's game who I think has "it." I first met Patrick at a college skills competition back at the Super Bowl in 2000, when he was still at Tulane. I was really impressed with him. He did very well in the competition—I thought he was head and shoulders above the rest of the quarterbacks there, even though no one had really heard a lot about him yet. But what struck me most about him was his charisma. He was very confident and yet very respectful of everyone who was working there.

Two years later, we were preparing for the telecast of a game between Washington and Tennessee, and I asked for Patrick to be brought into the production meetings so we could all talk to him. Danny Wuerffel was the starting quarterback for the Redskins, and Patrick, who wasn't supposed to play, hadn't even made his NFL debut yet, but I wanted the other guys to see what I meant about "it."

So we talked to him, and they all agreed, yes, we see what you mean. Then Wuerffel got hurt early in the game and Patrick came in for him. He passed for 268 yards and 2 touchdowns in his first NFL game, and he led the Redskins to a 31–14 victory on the road. Then the following week, I thought he was even more impressive. He was the starter against New Orleans and he really got roughed up. He was intercepted four times and sacked several other times, and the Saints built a 20–0 lead in the first half. But he hung in there and brought

Moose's Memories

Troy Aikman was the quarterback pretty much my whole career in Dallas. Steve Walsh played a little in my rookie year of 1989, and we had a few people come in for Troy here and there when he was banged up, but other than that, I always lined up behind Troy.

I'm biased, of course, but Troy was the best I ever saw. Nobody was better at throwing the ball in traffic, pinning the ball right on a receiver coming across the middle of the field. Or throwing the ball nearly two-thirds of the field, on a line, to a guy coming out of his break.

Troy was a tough guy, too. He was like a linebacker playing the quarterback position. I don't think people realize he was 6'4" tall and weighed 220 pounds. And he was a lot faster than people ever gave him credit for. He was very quick.

Troy had a lot of God-given ability. But he also had "it" as much as anybody I've ever met.

his team back. He passed for 320 yards and a touchdown and ran for another touchdown. Even though New Orleans got a punt return for a touchdown that sealed the game in the second half, he showed everybody what "it" is.

In the Huddle

A good quarterback commands respect in the huddle. In Dallas, when Troy Aikman would step out of the huddle to get the play from the coaches on the communication system, it was chaos in there. Michael Irvin felt nobody could cover him. Emmitt Smith just wanted to run the football. The offensive line wanted to blow everybody off the ball. Everybody would be shouting at once, "Why don't we do this?" or "Why don't we do that?"

And then as soon as Troy would step back into the huddle, you could hear a pin drop. It was his huddle, and he left no doubt about it. He had a presence. If you did something wrong, just one look from him was all it took, and you knew.

WATCHING FOOTBALL

NFL Ranking

The NFL ranks its quarterbacks by a complicated formula that considers percentage of passes completed, average yards per attempt, percentage of touchdown passes, and percentage of passes intercepted. It's an accurate reflection of a quarterback's passing ability. But it's not the complete picture for a quarterback. The formula cannot take into account the intangibles that separate the great ones from the rest of the field.

Whatever It Takes

A great quarterback makes all of his teammates better. In Dallas, for instance, Emmitt Smith became the NFL's all-time rushing leader, but I don't think that would have happened without Troy Aikman at quarterback. Troy could put his ego aside. His passing statistics are not on a par with some of the other great quarterbacks in history. But that's a huge credit to him, because our team never could have accomplished what it did—and that includes winning three Super Bowls in four years—if it had a quarterback who was driven by numbers.

We were a run-oriented team with a back who was on track to become the all-time leading rusher very early in his career, and we had a quarterback who said, "Fine. If that's what it is going to take to get us to the Super Bowl, then I'm all for it. I'll go 17 [completions] for 22 [attempts], 198 yards and 2 touchdowns. I don't need to throw the ball 35 or 40 times and pass for 3 or 4 touchdowns a game."

If fantasy football were as big in the 1990s as it is now, Troy probably would be way down on your list because he just didn't have those gaudy statistics. But another great thing about him was that if Emmitt was down or the other team had taken him out of the game, we could lean on Troy to throw 30 or 35 passes. He could throw for 300 yards and 3 touchdowns in a game if he had to.

It was kind of pick your poison with us—do you want us to beat you by running or passing, because we can do both—and I was always so impressed by Troy's approach. It was fun for me to be around a guy who all he wanted to do was win. It was never about the numbers.

It was all about winning championships, and I think that's a big reason we won three of them. He set the tone for our team.

One of the quarterbacks out there today who is a lot like Troy in that respect is Atlanta's Michael Vick. It's easy to see how important Michael is to the success of the Falcons. When he really hit the scene in 2002, Atlanta made the playoffs and was one of the NFL's most promising teams. Then he got hurt the next year, and the Falcons were terrible. He came back in 2004, and Atlanta went all the way to the NFC Championship Game.

But what a lot of people don't know is that Michael is one of those quarterbacks who only wants to win. He's a flashy player who can do amazing things on the field, but he is not driven by a desire to do it all himself or put up fancy statistics. He can have an off game, but as long as his team wins, that's what matters to him. You don't often see that in such a young guy.

Daryl's Best

Quarterbacks are all different, so it's hard to pick out one and say he's the best. You can't knock Indianapolis' Peyton Manning after the record-setting season he had in 2004. Tom Brady has proven he's a winner in New England, and ultimately that's what it's all about. Donovan McNabb has been a consistent winner in Philadelphia, too. Then there is Green Bay's Brett Favre. To me he's the guy out there who is a throwback. He's the last of the great group of quarterbacks from the 1990s, such as Dallas' Troy Aikman, San Francisco's Steve Young, Buffalo's Jim Kelly, and Denver's John Elway—guys who played on teams that were driven by the quarterback. And the way Brett is on the football field is the way he is when you meet him. When you sit down with him, you see how much fun he is. His approach is just the opposite of Troy Aikman's. Troy was so focused. Brett just stays so loose. He's fun to watch.

Reading Defenses

You can teach a quarterback to read defenses, that is, knowing what to expect from the defense based on the alignment and the personnel it is showing when you come up to the line of scrimmage. It's just like studying a book for a college course or learning a foreign language. Some quarterbacks will naturally pick it up a little bit quicker than others. And then it depends on how much effort they want to put into it. But there's also a limit now to how much you can get from a presnap read. It's become a lot more difficult today than it ever used to be—even as recently as ten years ago. That's because of the elaborate defensive schemes and the skills of the athletes playing defense and their ability to disguise things. They can disguise what they're going to do in lots of different ways to fool the quarterback as he steps to the ball. A defensive player might come into the box (the imaginary area near the line of scrimmage in which most of the defenders line up at the beginning of the play) like he's going to be an extra guy in run support, and then he still gets back in time to cover the deep pass. Philadelphia safety Brian Dawkins is one of those players. It amazes me how many looks he can give a quarterback at the line of scrimmage, and then get back into whatever his assignment is supposed to be on a given play.

The Zone Blitz and Pass Coverages

The zone blitz scheme has really challenged the quarterbacks' presnap reads. One of the ways that teams could always beat what the defense threw at them was with their hot adjustments. When a receiver saw two blitzers from his side going after the quarterback, he would adjust his route by running a flat or a slant or a stick route, a 5-yard hitch. But now the defense drops a defensive tackle or a defensive end right into that area. So the quarterback sees two blitzers when he makes his presnap read, only it's not really two blitzers because one of the defensive players is going to drop back out. It's really just a single blitz, and there's going to be a defender right in the lane where the hot read is going. (A hot read is a quick adjustment, this time by the quarterback and wide receiver who have recognized the overload blitz.) It all makes

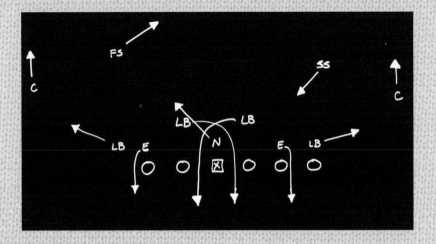

Gridiron Glossary

The **zone blitz** is the defense's response to the West Coast Offense. The defensive team appears to bring two blitzers just off the line of scrimmage to pressure the quarterback, only to have one drop back into a designated zone in pass coverage. When effective, this places a defender in an area of the field in which the quarterback expected to find no one. The defense looks as though it has too many players for the offense to block, but that is not the case. It is just a matter of sorting out where the five rushers are.

it a much bigger mental challenge for the quarterback. It can be very difficult on him.

The coverages a quarterback faces are different now, too. There used to be Cover 2 and Cover 3. Now you have Quarters or a Cover 4, which is essentially a four-deep coverage. You've got Quarter Halves, where half the field is being covered by two guys and the other half of the field is being manned by a single defensive player. You've got zones behind man-under schemes. Or Man Free, which is man-for-

Gridiron Glossary

Cover 2 is a basic pass defense in which each of the two safeties is responsible for one half of the defensive secondary.

Defenses used to play straight-up man-for-man coverage or use simple zones. Now they are more innovative. There are just so many different things that defenses can do nowadays that the quarterback's ability to figure it all out with a presnap read is more and more limited.

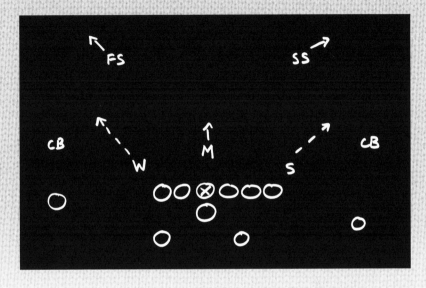

man coverage, except that the free safety lurks into an area where the defense thinks the ball is going to go, based on down and distance or the offensive grouping. Or defenses can use that free man to double cover the offense's big receiver, maybe helping out on a guy like the Philadelphia Eagles Terrell Owens on the outside or the New York Jets Wayne Chrebet in the slot.

On the Same Page

It's really fun to watch two guys in the passing game who have worked together for a long time. When I was with the Cowboys, I used to enjoy watching film with quarterback Troy Aikman and tight end Jay

Novacek. Troy joined the Cowboys in 1989, and Novacek the next season. They played together for six years, so each came to know what the other guy was going to do.

Because of the nature of my position, I knew how you were supposed to run all the tight end routes. We had one route that was a simple pattern: Go 10 to 12 yards off the line of scrimmage, then break in toward the middle of the field. It was a "4" on the passing tree. And you would always break across a man's face—run in front of him. And you never allowed the defender between you and the quarterback. If a defender had you in man-for-man coverage, you would cut across his face. That was just the rule in our offense. This way, the quarterback knew what the pass receiver was going to do. He knew the receiver was going to cross the defender's face. If the receiver went behind the defender instead, it could lead to an interception. So you never wanted him to go behind.

But sometimes we'd be watching film, and Jay would have the 4 route, and he would cut in behind the defender. But then Jay would come backward, and Troy already would have released the ball and have it there off the defender's back shoulder. I'd look at Jay and say, "Okay, how did you know the ball would be there for you off the defender's back shoulder? You didn't go across his face—you actually went behind him and pivoted back out." Jay would say, "Because that's where Troy always throws the ball." And I'd turn to Troy and say, "Why did you throw the ball there?" And Troy would say, "Because that's where Jay always comes back to."

These two had spent so many years together that each one knew what the other guy was going to do. And that made that route almost impossible to defend, because a defensive player looking at the play on film during the week sees that it can go three or four different ways. But only Troy and Jay know exactly what the other guy is going to do.

The trouble now is that I don't know if you can get to that point anymore. Certainly, you can't do it as much. So many guys come and go in free agency that it is tougher and tougher for players to develop that rapport.

Long Toss

The 18-yard in route and the 18-yard comeback to the opposite hash are the big-arm throws. When you see a quarterback who can make those passes, you know he's got an NFL-caliber arm. Troy Aikman could throw those passes as well as anybody who ever played the game.

On short crossing patterns, though, you don't want to see the ball drilled in there. A high, hard pass that bounces off a running back or a tight end's hands is very likely to be intercepted. You want to see a soft, catchable ball. Troy Aikman was great about that. I got an opportunity to play with Bernie Kosar when Troy went down one year, and I played with Steve Young at the Pro Bowl in Hawaii, but the touch that Troy could put on the ball really separated him from some of those other great quarterbacks.

In Sync

Sometimes it takes a while for a quarterback and a wide receiver to get in sync when one or the other (or both) are new to a team. I think that's what we expected in Philadelphia in 2004, when wide receiver Terrell Owens joined the Eagles and teamed with quarterback Donovan McNabb for the first time. We expected players like wide receiver Todd Pinkston and tight end Chad Lewis to get off to decent starts, and then eventually Terrell would start to make an impact as teams realized the Eagles had other weapons. But we broadcast the Eagles' opener against the New York Giants, and Terrell had three touchdown catches. And he was wide open on one of them. It was unbelievable. I mean, how do you lose track of Terrell Owens, especially in the red zone?

I think Donovan's ability to extend a play gives his team a chance to make positive yards even after a play breaks down or is well defended, and I think he and Terrell just developed a rapport faster than people ever thought they would. It was very impressive how quickly they got together on the same page.

Gridiron Glossary

The **red zone** is the area inside the defending team's 20 yard line. It's not an official term, but you'll often hear it used on television emphasizing the importance of coming away with points—at least a field goal but preferably a touchdown—whenever an offense penetrates that area of the field.

In Dallas we called it the "green zone" on offense. We had the ball, and we wanted to keep going—red for stop, green for go. It also is the area of the field where you make your money.

The Shotgun

Many NFL teams now have a version of the Shotgun Offense. In the shotgun, instead of taking the snap directly from the center, the quarterback lines up 3 to 5 yards behind the center and takes a long snap.

The advantage for the quarterback is that he has a better vantage point to survey the opposing defense and pick out a receiver. The disadvantage is that a defense pretty much knows that a pass is coming and can really get after the quarterback. Running from the shotgun might surprise the defense, but even then the running back is going up against a wall of rushers. Also you are limited to specific plays such as draws and shovel passes. For the shovel pass a quarterback moves toward the end of the line of scrimmage and flips the ball to the running back cutting underneath the quarterback. This is actually a pass play, and if the ball is dropped by the running back, it is not a fumble, it is an incomplete pass. In general most teams only go to the shotgun in obvious passing situations.

Another disadvantage for the quarterback in the shotgun that is sometimes overlooked is that he has to catch the ball. Instead of instinctively taking the snap like he does when under center, the

History Book

The shotgun's roots go back to the 1960 season, when Red Hickey was coaching the San Francisco 49ers. Hickey installed the shotgun late in his team's frustrating season, and the 49ers closed the year with four wins in five games. The next year, they traded quarterback Y. A. Tittle to the New York Giants and alternated John Brodie (a passer), Billy Kilmer (a runner), and Bobby Watters (a little of both) in the shotgun. And they opened the season with four wins in five games.

Unfortunately for Hickey and the 49ers, opposing teams quickly adjusted to the shotgun. The Chicago Bears aligned star linebacker Bill George on the line of scrimmage and beat San Francisco 31–0. The 49ers didn't win any of their next three games, either—and that was the end of their shotgun.

The 49ers eventually settled on Brodie as their primary starting quarterback, and he turned out to be a pretty good one. But in New York Tittle led the Giants to the NFL Championship Game three times in four seasons, and he wound up in the Pro Football Hall of Fame.

quarterback has to take his eyes off the defense, at least momentarily, to pick up the long snap. And the snap is not always perfect, either. It can be a little bit high, or a little low, or to the right or left. At best a poor snap will throw off the timing of the play a little bit. At worst it can result in disaster for the offense.

The Two-Minute Drill

The need for an effective two-minute drill is obvious. If a team is behind late in the game or wants to take advantage of a possession as the first half is winding down, it goes into hurry-up mode.

Gridiron Glossary

The **two-minute drill** (or "two-minute offense") is a quick-strike attack in which the offense usually utilizes passing plays and doesn't huddle between snaps. Plays are often called by the quarterback at the line of scrimmage. It is so called because it's most often used in the final two minutes of the game or of the first half, but it is occasionally used at other times in the game by a team that is looking for a spark that a change of pace can provide.

Sometimes teams move up and down the field at will during the two-minute drill, and fans wonder why on earth they don't just stick with it all the time. The reason is that the defense is not going to use a lot of the elaborate schemes that they would employ during the rest of the game. Usually the defense will go to a prevent defense in which the defensive secondary will play their coverages (predominately zone coverages) deeper, to prevent the big play. Many people believe, myself included, that prevent defenses prevent you from winning because they often allow large chunks of yardage in exchange for taking time off the clock.

In Dallas we worked on the two-minute drill a lot in training camp. Then, once the season started, Thursday was the practice day during which we worked on it. Generally, teams will have specific plays that they run in the two-minute drill, things they are comfortable with. They might throw in a new wrinkle once in a while, but they will pretty much be the same plays.

A lot of times in the two-minute drill at the end of the first half or in a tie game, teams will begin with something safe—a short screen pass or a draw—just to see if it can make any positive yards right off the bat. If that works, then all of a sudden things will start to pick up. And if the drill doesn't produce the results a coach wants, then he might turn around and say, "Okay, let's sit on it and let the clock run." One of the most obvious examples of that thought process came at the end of Super Bowl XXXVI in the 2001 season, when the Patriots and the Rams were tied. New England had the ball in its own territory in a tie game, and most viewers figured that they would run out the clock and go to overtime. But Patriots coach Bill Belichick and his offensive coordinator Charlie Weis (now the head coach at Notre Dame) knew that the Rams didn't have any time-outs left, so he figured he could run a couple of safe plays, and if it didn't look as if it was going to work out, then he could sit on the ball. So, if you remember, quarterback Tom Brady dumped off a few short passes to running back J. R. Redmond early in that drive. Then, when the Patriots got a first down or two out of that, they decided to go for it. The end result was the game-winning field goal.

Sometimes teams go into a hurry-up mode earlier in the game just to take advantage of a personnel grouping that the defense has on the field. And once the offense has surprised the defense with that, it wants to keep it going and keep the ball in play to keep the defense from bringing in different players to adjust.

Daryl's Best

There may never have been a player better at running the two-minute drill than Denver's Hall of Fame quarterback John Elway. In his career Elway directed the Broncos to many come-from-behind victories, often in the closing minutes or in overtime. In January 1987 he led the Broncos on a 98-yard drive to the tying touchdown against Cleveland in the AFC Championship Game. That march, under such pressure and on the road, was so dramatic that if you talk about "The Drive," everyone knows that's what you mean.

Among current quarterbacks Indianapolis' Peyton Manning is certainly one of the best at running the two-minute drill. And for a young player Jacksonville's Byron Leftwich has already had a couple of pretty good comebacks in his career. And then there is Atlanta's Michael Vick. We did one Falcons game last season against the Saints in which Vick needed about 55 yards in the two-minute drill. He needed just two plays to get those yards. Now that was impressive.

The Mobile Quarterback

A mobile quarterback gives an offense an added dimension that can really make things tough on a defense. The Falcons Michael Vick just absolutely frightens defensive coordinators because of his ability to take off and run when everything else breaks down around him. That's something that a defense just can't account for. A coach does the best he can, but even if a defense has every receiver covered, a player like Vick or Minnesota's Daunte Culpepper or Philadelphia's Donovan McNabb can make something out of the play.

On the flip side of that, some mobile quarterbacks always think they can make something out of nothing. A lot of teams have something called a "scramble drill." When the players running their pass routes see the quarterback start moving around the pocket, the short receivers usually go deep, and the deep receivers come back. The important thing is just to keep moving, try to get to an open area

Rules to Know

The NFL has liberalized intentional grounding rules:

1. An eligible receiver (wide receiver, running back, or tight end) only needs to be in the vicinity of the intended pass.

2. Outside the pocket the quarterback only needs to advance the ball beyond the line of scrimmage.

Penalties for roughing the quarterback have been strengthened:

1. Two-step rule—once the pass is thrown, a defender cannot take two or more steps and hit the quarterback.

2. A defender cannot slam the quarterback into the ground.

Defensive players cannot hit the quarterback in the head or at or below the knees.

somewhere. But the quarterback can't try to ad-lib too much. Sometimes there just comes a point when it's simply a dead play: This play is not going to work. The quarterback must understand that he can't let anything bad happen, like an ill-advised pass that is intercepted, and they simply move on to the next play.

As backfield mates Emmitt Smith and I developed great chemistry. That quality existed throughout our team and was a cornerstone to our success during our Super Bowl Championship teams of the '90s.

Photo courtesy of the *Dallas Cowboys Official Weekly*

CHAPTER ELEVEN

Running Backs

Vision and Balance

Running backs are the players who line up in the offensive backfield behind the quarterback. The positions that make up the running backs are the H-back, the fullback, and the halfback. The halfback is the position that has assumed the generic name of running back.

A lot of what it takes to play running back is simply natural, God-given ability. But then it's vision and balance, too. Great vision allows a running back to see any potential tackler coming in pursuit, and great balance allows the running back to make radical cuts to avoid the tackle or to stay on his feet when most would go to the ground. It's the ability to make defensive players miss him. And when he can't make them miss, he just tries to run over them. It's running in the open field and it's running physically between the tackles. And a good running back helps his team out in the passing game, too, not just by catching passes but also by protecting the quarterback.

Gridiron Glossary

An **H-back** is a player whose role is a combination of a tight end and a fullback. This position became popular in the 1980s in Washington with Joe Gibbs's Redskins. The H-back will line up in the traditional tight-end or fullback positions and will also be involved in motions in the offensive backfield. With Joe Gibbs's return to the NFL and the success of Redskins H-back Chris Cooley last year, more teams may begin to use the H-back.

Moose's Memories

When Cowboys running back Emmitt Smith was in his prime, he'd do things I'd never seen before on film. Come Monday I'd be sitting next to him in the meeting room watching film. And I'd be saying, "Emmitt, how did you do that?" Then two weeks later, he'd do something else I had never seen before on film. And it was, "How did you do that?" It was almost a weekly thing with him.

Emmitt was a complete player. He was a great runner, of course, but he also was a very good pass protector, for which I don't think he's ever really gotten enough credit. And he was a very good receiver, too.

Emmitt retired after the 2004 season with 18,355 career rushing yards, the most in NFL history. He had surpassed Walter Payton's mark of 16,726 yards while still in Dallas in 2002, then played his final two seasons for the Arizona Cardinals. Now everyone wants to know, "Who is going to be the back that passes Emmitt?" But I don't know if anyone is going to be able to go ten or twelve years—even a ten-year career means gaining 1,800 yards a season—and catch him. Even if a guy takes it to fifteen years, can anyone stay healthy that long with as physical as the game is now? I think that's what will separate Emmitt from anyone chasing him.

The Great Ones

A great running back has tremendous peripheral vision. It's something I heard Tony Dorsett confirm. Dorsett, a Pro Football Hall of Fame running back who played for the Cowboys and Broncos in his twelve-year career from 1977 to 1988, said he could see where everybody else was on the field. Curtis Martin, the great Jets running back—at age thirty-one in 2004, he became the oldest player ever to win an NFL rushing title—says that he sees everyone in terms of colors. He sees flashes of uniform colors. But it is essentially the same thing. These guys have great peripheral vision, so they always know where their blockers are and where the potential tacklers are lurking.

Jim Brown, the former Cleveland great, was a big, physical running back with tremendous breakaway speed. Then there was Franco Harris, who helped the Steelers win a bunch of championships, and

Barry Sanders, who could take what appeared to be a sure 3-yard loss and turn it into a 5-yard gain—you can go right down the list. It really becomes a personal thing when you consider who's the best in this position. But I think what really sets apart a couple of backs, Walter Payton and Emmitt Smith, is, number one, their longevity—their ability to play as long as they did and to stay relatively injury free—and, number two, their passion for the game.

Before the Snap

You hear coaches and analysts talk all the time about the importance of the presnap read for the quarterback, but I think that presnap is important for a running back as well. You always want to know where your run support is. You'll learn as much as you can even before you take the field by studying tape during the week. You want to know the strengths and weaknesses of your offensive linemen. Is a guy a good zone blocker? Is he a good trapper? How well does he match up against the guy he's going against today? Do they anticipate your cutbacks?

No Big Hits

When you have a running back with the great vision and the great balance, and then he puts in that extra film study, too, then you have the "complete package." Emmitt Smith had tremendous balance—he could stay on his feet after taking hits when he should have gone right down. And maybe nobody was better at that than Barry Sanders. I've seen defensive players walking back toward the huddle thinking that Barry was tackled, then all of a sudden he's gone, heading downfield.

Another of Emmitt's great talents was that he never seemed to take that big hit. I think that's one of the reasons that he had such a long career. I don't know if too many running backs, especially when you talk about those big, physical, punishing runners, can last beyond ten years anymore. Take a guy like Earl Campbell—Houston Oilers head coach Bum Phillips rode him until he broke. Earl didn't avoid tackles, he took them on. I just don't know if you can dish out—and take—that kind of punishment on a weekly basis and hang in there.

You hear players get called out, criticized because they're running

History Book

down the sidelines, and then they step out of bounds instead of taking another hit. To me, that's fine. Live to play another day. Obviously, you'd love to have a guy lower his shoulder and turn it back in, but I leave that up to them. Let them make their own decisions about what's best for them and best for their team.

In the middle of the field, of course, you don't have that option. You've got all those players converging on you from all directions. But the good running back will never take that really big hit. You really don't often see a running back take a hard shot in the field of play like the receiver sometimes does. The running back relies on his vision to make a cut or spin move and avoid the big physical hit.

It's a Thinking Game

For me the mental aspect of the game was most important—studying, knowing what to watch on film. Knowing about the guy you're going up against. Knowing what a player struggles with against a blocker, what he doesn't like. Most defenders hate being cut. A cut block is a block where you put your shoulder right through the thigh pad of your blocking assignment. When a cut block is done correctly, the first thing that hits the ground is the defender's head. And even if it is not a perfect block, it gives the defender something to think about the rest of the game.

Gridiron Glossary

A **cut block** is a low block in which an offensive player initiates the block into the thigh of the defender. If he initiates the block too low, today's defenders are so athletic that they will simply jump over him or stuff him head first into the turf.

First, you always want to cut a defensive player early in the game, just to see what his reaction is going to be to it. And second, you've got to do it just so he knows that he can't come up and try to blow you up all the time, that he can't try to knock you on your butt every play. So every once in a while, you go up to him and you just chop him down. You always like to send that message early in the game.

Still, you have to be selective when you're going to cut a guy. In Dallas Emmitt Smith had tremendous confidence in his blockers. He expected the running lane to be there and then he would explode into the secondary. But if I came up and cut a guy in the hole, there would be no hole for Emmitt to go through.

The Physics of Football

I always liked to use an opponent's momentum to block him. My running backs coach would tell me that I had to take the defensive player right down the middle so the running back behind me could decide which way was best for him to go. But I always thought it was easier, when a guy was scraping into the hole from my right to left, to try to take his right shoulder and wheel him. I'd push him past the hole instead of taking him straight down the middle and trying to stop his momentum and redirect him. I was just using a little bit of physics. It's a lot more difficult to stop a 240-pound guy and redirect all of his momentum than it is to utilize that momentum to carry him past the hole.

You get a feel for it. You learn whether you can stay up on your opponent or whether you can cut him. But the thing that helped me the most was playing so long with Emmitt Smith and coming to know his running style, knowing when he was going to stay playside (where the play is designed to go) or when he was going to cut to the back side (the opposite side of where the play is designed to go).

By our third or fourth year, Emmitt Smith and I were moving in a synchronized motion. We started to read the developing play in unison, and I could come out the back door with him, knowing he would be thinking about cutting back. Or I knew when he wanted to stay playside and bounce (move to the outside).

Double Trouble

A back who can catch the ball coming out of the backfield can create tremendous problems for a defense. Look at Brian Westbrook in Philadelphia. When we talk to defensive coordinators around the league for our telecasts, Westbrook is their biggest worry. They are really concerned about him—and not necessarily as a runner. They know that with everyone else going down the field, quarterback Donovan McNabb can just dump off the ball to Westbrook, and he's got lots of room to maneuver—say, 15 yards of space and just one defender in there. That's just not a good situation for a defense to be in. Green Bay learned that last year when Brian caught 3 touchdown passes against them. In a game against the New York Giants, he took a little dump-off pass from McNabb and scooted 34 yards through the defense for a touchdown.

A running back who can catch the ball just gives an offense another weapon. If a team has only one legitimate threat on offense, a defense can take that guy away, whether it's a running back, a wide receiver, or a tight end. There are things a defense can do from a schematic standpoint to keep that player from doing too much damage. But if a team has two threats—or if it gets to the point where it has three real threats—now the defense is in trouble.

Moose's Memories

The media liked to call our big stars on offense in Dallas the "Triplets": quarterback Troy Aikman, running back Emmitt Smith, and wide receiver Michael Irvin. But we also could hurt opposing defenses with wide receiver Alvin Harper and tight end Jay Novacek. In our situation, what were opposing teams going to do? Were they going to crowd the line of scrimmage and bring an eighth guy in close to try to stop Emmitt? Okay, then that meant they were in single coverage against Michael, Jay, or Alvin on the outside. And we were happy to take our chances one-on-one with those guys whenever teams wanted to try that. Anytime you can threaten a defense with multiple options, you have a great chance to be successful.

That's what the St. Louis Rams did to their opponents in 1999. They could do so many things on the offensive side of the ball that they came to be known as the "Greatest Show on Turf." Which wide receiver were teams going to cover: Isaac Bruce, Torry Holt, Az-Zahir Hakim, or Ricky Proehl? The Rams were saying, "Our third and fourth wide receivers are better than your nickel or dime back." That was their mentality. There always was a mismatch. And then, once they really had a defense dazed and confused, they could always turn

Gridiron Glossary

Nickel Back, Dime Back

Since a base defense features four defensive backs, when a team brings in an extra defensive back in passing situations, the fifth member of the secondary is called a nickel back. Sometimes, in obvious passing downs or against predominately passing teams, you'll even find two nickel backs on the field. The second one is called the dime back (because two nickels equal a dime, of course!). If you hear an announcer tell you the defense is in a nickel package, you know it has five defensive backs on the field; a dime package means there are six.

around and hand the ball off to Marshall Faulk. That's an offense that's got something really special going. St. Louis scored 526 points that year and then 540 the next—the third most in a season in NFL history. The 1999 squad won Super Bowl XXXIV, 23–16, over Tennessee. The winning points came on a 73-yard touchdown pass from quarterback Kurt Warner to wide receiver Isaac Bruce with less than two minutes remaining in the game.

Fullbacks

The role of the fullback, or factor back as Merrill Hodge of ESPN so aptly calls him, in the running game is basically as a blocker. So for a fullback to get opportunities for touches (getting his hands on the ball) in the passing game, the more he knows about the passing game the better off he'll be and the better off the team will be. The team will be able to break formation, to get out of the I or the offset I, and put the fullback in the slot. Or on the outside to match up the fullback with a linebacker or safety and create more opportunities in the passing game.

I recognized early in my career that if I was ever going to have a chance to touch the ball, I was going to have to know the responsibilities of the receivers across the board. And because we were never really four deep at wide receiver, I didn't have to come off the field a lot. The coaches had enough confidence in me to create a favorable matchup against a safety or a linebacker. They figured we were better off in that situation than bringing in another wide receiver to go against one of the other team's nickel backs.

To me that's a better way for teams to do it, but I am biased. If a team leaves its fullback and regular personnel on the field, then all of a sudden shifts and moves the fullback into the slot or splits him out wide to either side, then that puts a lot of pressure on the defense. First of all, there's still a lot of uncertainty on the defense's part when the offense breaks the huddle. The defense sees you haven't gone three wide—bringing in a third wide receiver—yet, or even four wide, so they still have to worry about whether you're going to run the ball or do any of a number of different things. And now the offense can pass the ball or come out and still run the ball. Or maybe the defense anticipated a power running play coming out of the huddle. But now, after shifting into a passing formation using the fullback where a wide receiver would normally line up, the offense can really cross them up.

Catching the Football

You learn to catch a football just by doing it. I got my pass-catching ability as a kid playing in the backyard. In college I didn't catch the ball a whole lot. I only had 46 receptions in my whole career at Syracuse. Then in Dallas one year (1993), I caught 50 passes.

It was easy for me to catch the ball. Everyone knows how to do that. But the big thing that I learned in Dallas was how to run routes. I was in tight end Jay Novacek's ear all the time, looking for advice, learning things. One time, he told me something about route running that I'll never forget. He said it's not how fast you run that matters, it's how fast you stop. That was what I learned watching Jay run his pass routes. Defenders could keep with him stride for stride all through his route. But when he broke off his route, that's where he created separation from the defender.

I was in the same boat; I was never going to outrun anybody. But I worked with Jay and I learned some subtle things about the underneath routes—those typically run by tight ends and running backs, or even by a wide receiver all the way across the field. But most important, I learned how to create separation by getting out of the routes quicker than the man covering me. I knew where I was going and he didn't.

Blocking

The number one thing about blocking is the whole mentality of it. You know it's not fun, so you have to put yourself in the right frame of mind. And by the nature of your position, you know going in that it's not a very glamorous job.

It also becomes an ego thing. You don't want to be blocking a player who is always the one who's making the tackle. One year, when the Cowboys played New England, it seemed as if Ted Johnson, the Patriots excellent linebacker, made every tackle on the first six or seven plays of the game. Finally, Emmitt Smith came back to huddle all ticked off and said, "Who's got number 52?" It turned out it was someone different on almost every play. You just don't want to be that guy everyone sees missing the block in the film room on Monday after the game.

Every defensive player has a different style. You just have to get used to it. A linebacker like Eric Hill of the Cardinals was one of those guys I had to cut early every week we played against him. You can't let a guy who is that big come to the hole so fast every time. And I was doing it for my own self-preservation. I didn't want to have to butt heads with him on every play.

Moose's Memories

The toughest guy for me to block in my career was Eric Hill—without a doubt. Eric was a linebacker who came into the league the same year that I did (1989). He played his first nine seasons with the Cardinals, who were in the same division as the Cowboys then, so we played them twice a year. But even before that, in my senior year of college, Syracuse (my school) played Louisiana State (Hill's school) in a bowl game. One of the most violent collisions I ever heard was between Eric and a guy who probably was the best guard on our team. I went through the hole as a lead blocker and heard this sickening thud behind me. I turned around and both Eric and the guard were on their backs. When we got back to Syracuse, I had to go look at the film because I wanted to see who it was that did it. It was Eric, and when he and the guard went at it, it was like two rams butting heads on a hillside.

Then Eric got drafted by the Cardinals, and I got drafted by Dallas. The Cardinals moved him from outside linebacker to inside linebacker. And because our offense was pretty basic when we played the Cardinals—a heavy dose of strong-side leads—Eric and I went head to head a lot of times over the years.

Eric was one of the first of the physical run stoppers who also was very athletic. He could cover guys in the passing game, too. Seth Joyner of the Eagles was another guy who was athletic enough to make you miss him, but also strong enough to knock you on your butt. So he gave you a different challenge each week.

There is a lot of discussion about who is the best player at certain positions, but at wide receiver there is no doubt. Jerry Rice is, was, and always will be the best wide receiver to play the game.

Photo by Terrell Lloyd, 49ers staff photographer

CHAPTER TWELVE

Wide Receivers and Tight Ends

The Men Who Catch the Ball

A pass catcher capable of making plays down the field can make all the difference in the world to an offense. He opens up the running game and takes pressure off the quarterback, placing it squarely on the opposing team, making it defend more areas of the field.

Look at Philadelphia in 2004: As fantastic a quarterback as Donovan McNabb is, until the Eagles obtained big-play wide receiver Terrell Owens before the season, they were always good, but not quite good enough. With Owens the team finally reached the Super Bowl his first season in Philadelphia.

In Dallas we had excellent wide receivers in Michael Irvin and Alvin Harper most of my time there. But we also had a tight end who was very involved in the passing game: Jay Novacek, a player who taught me a great deal about catching passes.

The Tight End

A tight end must be a good receiver and a good blocker. He is critical in the underneath passing game and a key element in the strong-side (to the tight end) running game. Some tight ends make their living in the passing game, like Tony Gonzalez or Jeremy Shockey, and others are key to the running game, like Ernie Conwell. You have a special guy when he can do both. Mark Bavaro was a complete tight end. His blocking was critical to the running game, and as a receiver, he was essential in the passing game.

How many passes the tight end catches depends a great deal on the system in which he plays. Some teams prefer to keep the tight end in to block as much as possible instead of going out for a pass. He becomes an extra blocker in pass protection. Or perhaps a team does not have a strong or a healthy offensive line and needs the tight end to help keep the opposing pass rush from getting to the quarterback. On the other hand, teams that don't have experienced or big-play wide receivers or just want to give a young quarterback a big target in the middle of the field might rely on the tight end—typically at 6'4" or more—to catch passes more frequently. And some teams have a pair of tight ends who split the roles: one guy who is the primary pass catcher and another guy who is more of a designated blocker.

Jay Novacek averaged 56 catches a season for Dallas from 1990 to 1995. That's more than a lot of number two wide receivers. And in 2004 Jason Witten set Cowboys' records for a tight end by catching 87 passes for 980 yards.

Wide Receivers

The wide receivers are the big play threats on the offensive side of the ball. Size and speed are coveted by coaches, but the ability to catch the ball in traffic and make yards after the catch separates the

History Book

A couple of NFL tight ends had record-breaking seasons in 2004. In Kansas City the Chiefs Tony Gonzalez caught 102 passes—he was the first tight end in NFL history to break the century mark in one season. And in San Diego Antonio Gates caught 13 touchdown passes. That's more than any other tight end in league history caught in one season. Gates is an interesting story. He didn't play football when he went to college at Kent State. He played basketball instead. But the 6'4", 260-pounder gives quarterback Drew Brees a big target. (And maybe there's something to that basketball experience—the 6'4" Gonzalez played on the hardwood and the gridiron in his college days at California!)

Moose's Memories

Without a doubt there was nobody in Dallas who worked harder than Michael Irvin. Michael always felt he wasn't as talented as Jerry Rice or that he didn't have as much natural ability as someone like Herman Moore of Detroit or some of the other wide receivers who were playing during that era. And so he would just go and outwork them. That's why I never could believe some of the stuff that people were saying about Michael's lifestyle. There's simply no way that you can have that kind of a lifestyle away from the locker room and then come back and work that hard.

good from the great. Some wide receivers are considered big play types such as Randy Moss and Terrell Owens. From any point on the field, they can go the distance. Others are possession receivers such as Wayne Chrebet of the Jets. He may not go over the top for 80 yards, but he will keep converting third downs, giving his team another set of downs and more opportunities to score.

Wide receivers are a little like quarterbacks in that they have to have a bit of an edge to them. They walk that fine line sometimes between confidence and arrogance. A lot of folks used to call Cowboys wide receiver Michael Irvin arrogant. I don't think he was arrogant. I just think he was flashy and showy. It was a little bit of an act with him. Just some individual marketing.

Jerry Rice, the best receiver in the history of the game, is a great guy. Lynn Swann, the Steelers' Hall of Fame receiver, is a great guy. The common denominators in all the great receivers like Irvin, Rice, and Swann, though, were tremendous confidence in their abilities and a desire to work hard. And they wanted the ball in their hands when there was an opportunity for a critical play in the game.

Fishing for Complements

If all an offense has is one guy to catch the ball, then defenses—and defensive coaches—are smart enough today to take away that guy without weakening themselves somewhere else on the field. So teams really need to find that complementary wide receiver to take some of the pressure off their main target.

Think back to the great Steelers teams of the 1970s. They had John Stallworth to go along with Lynn Swann. The 49ers of the 1980s had John Taylor to complement Jerry Rice. In Dallas we had Alvin Harper with Michael Irvin. Now, I wouldn't put Alvin in the same class as Stallworth or Taylor. You saw what happened when he went to Tampa Bay—he wasn't cut out to be a number one wide receiver. But sometimes a guy has to know his role. And Alvin knew his in Dallas. He was a great complementary receiver. He wasn't the greatest route runner in the world. But he could run all day long. And if you ever went to sleep on him, he could go over the top on you in a heartbeat.

Total Effort on Every Play

Every receiver should run every route as if he's the primary guy on the play because you never know when the ball is coming to you. When I caught 50 passes for Dallas in 1993, I got my 50th catch of the season in the last game of the year, in overtime at New York against the Giants. It was the only time the ball ever had been thrown to me on that particular route. I was the fourth option in the quarterback's progression, a throwaway on the back side. It proved to me that you can't be out there loafing. You've got to come hard off the ball and get your head snapped around to pick up the flight of the ball.

It's All in the Release

For the wide receiver it's all in his release off the line of scrimmage. If he's being covered man for man, he needs to beat the defender coming off the line. The last thing he wants, from an offensive perspective, is contact. That disrupts his timing and gets him knocked out of his stem (the vertical aspect of the passing tree—every route comes off the vertical stem). And if a guy does get knocked off his route, it's very important that he get back on top of the defender and into that stem so the cover guy is trailing him. The receiver doesn't want the defender running shoulder to shoulder with him.

Moose's Memories

Our offense in Dallas was so precise that a certain foot forward or back, or the inside foot forward or the outside foot forward, was necessary on certain routes in order that the timing be correct. But because of that, the opponents' defensive backs could study film and have a pretty good idea that from this alignment or from that stance, the receiver only had a few possible routes to run. So defenses created problems from our perspective by learning to kind of sit on the curl or slant—depending on the alignment—and not worry about the hitch. After a while, then, we started making adjustments and doing things a little bit differently to confuse our opponents.

That's one of the great strengths Philadelphia's Terrell Owens has. He's so big and physical that he can get on top of the guys covering him. And once he does that, then he can break inside, or outside, or keep going.

Downfield Blocking

On running plays the wide receiver has to know that the ball can come back to him at any time. Just because he's lined up on the right and the running play is designed to go to the left doesn't necessarily mean it's not coming back to him. Think about a team like Detroit when the Lions had Barry Sanders, with his ability to improvise, or Dallas, where Emmitt Smith was such a great cutback runner, and you'll see what I mean. So, if the play is going away from the wide receiver, he still has to make sure to come off the ball (to release as if he's going to be the receiver and not jog off the line of scrimmage). The art of blocking by a wide receiver really has come back in the NFL these days. Coaches are really starting to stress to their players that they aren't out there just to catch the ball. When a running play is called, they need to be in on that, too, and be ready to block as well. We've gone into meetings as part of our game preparation during the week and the coaches tell us, "You've got to watch this guy block on the outside. He's awesome."

If a wide receiver has man-for-man coverage on him, sometimes the easiest block is just to release hard off the line of scrimmage and run off the defender. He is going to turn his back to the line and run with the receiver because he thinks he is running a pass route—and this allows the receiver to take his opponent right out of the play. That's when it's important for a receiver to know what kind of defense the opponent is in during presnap. If he sees it's not man coverage but zone, then he knows he's got to get to the defender's inside and get between him and the ballcarrier.

Daryl's Best

When it comes to wide receivers, I like to look for the complete player. A complete wide receiver is going to be able to catch the ball in all kinds of situations, run routes well, block downfield, and stay involved even when the play is not to him.

Oakland's Randy Moss, is he a complete wide receiver? No. He's probably the biggest scoring threat, sure. If you need a guy at that position to make a big play, I go with him. He may be the best in the game today.

Philadelphia's Terrell Owens is maybe a little more of an all-around player. He's got great size and he likes to block. A lot of his big plays come after the catch on the move. I don't put him up there with the best route runners, with the guys who run really precise routes. At the top of Terrell's routes, sometimes it's difficult for a quarterback to know exactly what Owens is going to do because he takes a little bit of creative license.

Indianapolis' Marvin Harrison is the most solid among today's wide receivers, without a doubt. He's probably the best route runner of the group, and probably the most dependable. He's got sneaky speed and great hands—certainly the best of the elite receivers currently playing. I really like Pittsburgh's Hines Ward, too. He's been underappreciated throughout his career, but he ranks among the best wide receivers in the game today.

Almost all a game's long runs come as the result of wide receivers blocking downfield (blocking players in the secondary, or defensive backfield). It might be a 15-yard run that suddenly turns into a 75-yard touchdown run because there were a couple of wide receivers working hard downfield.

Philadelphia's Terrell Owens is one of the really good blockers among the wide receivers today. All the guys from the Patriots are very good downfield blockers. Pittsburgh's Hines Ward is an excellent blocker, probably the best among the wide receivers playing now.

What the Receiver Needs to Recognize

The biggest thing for a wide receiver is knowing the difference between the two different types of defense, man and zone, before the ball is snapped. And then he needs to recognize where the defensive pressure is coming from. Is the defense bringing two blitzers from his side? If so, the line isn't going to be able to pick that up or block that scheme, so he has to know that he is now the hot receiver and has to cut short or adjust his route. Or if the defense zone blitzes, where two players start to come but one drops back, now the wide receiver has to know that the line should be able to successfully block the defense's pass rush because it's not an overload situation, so he can run his normal route. To me that's the hardest thing for a receiver—recognizing things in the defense's blitz package even more than recognizing its coverage.

Then there are the subtle things. For instance, if it's third and 13, and the route that is called in the huddle is designed to go 12 yards, the quarterback might say "sticks" or "chains," indicating that the receiver needs to stretch it out. In that case the receiver has to adjust his route a yard farther, or 2 or 3, whatever the case may be, so that if he makes the catch and gets tackled immediately, he still gets the first down. That's why so many of the best receivers always seem to get just to the first-down marker. And how many other times do we watch a game and say, "What is the point of throwing a 6-yard pass on third and 8?"

Communication is vital to the overall success of the offensive line. Dallas center Al Johnson makes sure everybody is on the same page.

Photo courtesy of the *Dallas Cowboys Official Weekly*

The Offensive Line

In It Together

You'll hear a lot of coaches say that if you win a game in the
trenches—along the offensive and defensive lines—you'll win on the
scoreboard. I think there's a lot of truth to that, and maybe more
validity than ever before. If you really want an indication of how well
a team is going to do, watch how the offensive line performs.

The offensive line consists of two tackles, two guards, and a center.
The tackles are the most athletic of the group. They must block the
athletic pass rushers playing on the outside of the defensive front
seven. The guards and center are very similar in stature and mentality—tough, physical players who are the key to any team with a good
running game. The offensive line is the group that takes the longest
to get used to playing with each other. Think about it: It's the only
area of the field where a player is shoulder to shoulder with another
player, and a lot of a guy's success depends on what the player next to
him is doing. The teams that keep their offensive lines together, or
keep them healthy over the course of a given season, are the teams
that have the most success. They are also often the teams that turn
out to be better than people expected at the beginning of the year.

When you see teams that have trouble staying healthy on the
offensive line, those are the teams that are going to have problems.
As players get hurt and have to sit out games, the skills of their
replacements aren't familiar to the rest of the line. This means they
are less likely to be able to run the ball or protect the quarterback
effectively. Free agency also has a negative impact on the offensive

line's chemistry. It has reduced the depth at every position, but it seems more so on the offensive line.

Look at the Baltimore Ravens: Jamal Lewis rushed for 2,066 yards in 2003. Then in 2004 he only got about half of that total—1,006 yards. He missed a couple of games to injury, but then he also was held to fewer than 100 yards in eight games. The difference? His offensive line was healthy in 2003, and it was in disarray in 2004. Mike Flynn, who started all sixteen games at center in 2003, got hurt early in the year, and the Ravens had a new center. Jonathan Ogden, the best tackle in the game, was in and out of the lineup after starting every game the year before. The new line just didn't have time to build good chemistry.

The Rams were another example in 2004. They were expected to win the division title, but they struggled much of the year. Well, they lost their starting center and their starting right tackle, and their offensive line was a shambles all year long. On the flip side the offensive lines of the Eagles and the Patriots stayed relatively healthy, and those two teams went to the Super Bowl.

Moose's Memories

I was fortunate enough to have played behind a bunch of really good offensive linemen in Dallas. Guard Larry Allen was probably the best of them. When he was in his prime, he did things you never expected to see from anybody in the NFL. Tackle Erik Williams was as mean as anybody I ever played with. He blocked Pro Football Hall of Fame defensive end Reggie White one-on-one at a time when not a whole lot of people were doing that. I don't know how many sacks Erik ever gave up to Reggie, but I know we played Green Bay in a lot of big games when Erik pitched a shutout at him. Mark Tuinei was a very big, very athletic left tackle. And Mark Stepnoski was an excellent center who coordinated all the protections up front. He was undersized, but he was such a great technician. He'd go up against a defensive tackle like Ted Washington and give up one hundred pounds, but he'd still do more than hold his own.

Domino Effect

Every team has injuries. And a lot of the time, a club gets hit hard in a particular area. When that happens, you need to look at what ripple effect it's going to have. And when the injuries happen to a team's offensive line, there's much more of a ripple.

Let's say a club loses its starting wideout (wide receiver). Maybe it's even a big playmaker, like Randy Moss. Minnesota lost him for a few weeks to injury last year and still was competitive, even against good teams such as Indianapolis and Green Bay, where the games were tied in the fourth quarter. Sometimes an opposing defense is going to really commit and take that star wide receiver out of the game, anyway. So a team is occasionally going to go without his production and has to learn to deal with it.

But teams can't go without a good effort and consistent play from their offensive line. They lose one guy, maybe they can hold off. They can do some things to help, like keep a tight end on the line or a running back in the backfield to help with pass protection. But once a team loses two regulars on the line, it's in trouble. And if it ever gets to the point where three players go down, well, there's just not a whole lot you can do about it.

Washington had a terrible time offensively in 2004. The Redskins ranked near the bottom of the league in total yards per game and in points scored. And a lot of the heat was directed at Mark Brunell, the quarterback, and Clinton Portis, the running back. But it's not fair to blame them. Look what happened to their offensive line. Tackle Jon Jansen went down in the preseason. Then Chris Samuels, another tackle, was injured.

When the players up front are injured, the running back doesn't know what their replacements are going to do. He's become accustomed to the strengths and weaknesses of his regular blockers. And he has a pretty good idea where he's going to take the ball because he knows those guys in front of him. But when a new starter comes in, the learning process starts all over again.

Rules to Know

Illegal Touching

Guards, centers, and tackles are not eligible to catch passes (except in fairly rare cases in which the tackle is not flanked on the outside by another player on his team and reports to the referee as an eligible receiver). Sometimes a pass will inadvertently hit one of the offensive linemen, and he'll throw up his hands as if to say, "I didn't mean to!" Intent has nothing to do with it, though. He still touched the ball, and it's still a penalty. A small rule change allows a defensive player to intercept the ball on the deflection. No longer is it a dead ball when touched by an offensive lineman.

Center of Attention

When you watch a football game on television, you'll often see the center pointing to players across the line of scrimmage or calling signals to his line mates. A lot of times the offensive line has its protection geared to a certain guy on the defense, so the center is calling out where that guy is. Maybe the protection is geared to the middle linebacker, but he's not actually lined up in the middle. The center sees that he's lined up over the tackle instead, so the center makes sure everybody knows where he is.

Or maybe the center sees a defensive lineman who has become a stand-up guy (playing like a linebacker) instead of a down lineman (on the line of scrimmage). And that's something the center's seen on film before so he's just pointing it out to his teammates. Say you have Philadelphia's Jevon Kearse, a defensive lineman, who is lined up in a two-point stance as a linebacker. The center points out that here's number 93, he's normally a down guy. But even though he's in a two-point stance at the linebacker level, the backs are not responsible for him, the line is. Everybody on the line knows they have to account for number 93. It's just a way of alerting guys to the proper scheme for protecting the quarterback.

Gridiron Glossary

A **protection scheme** is the blocking assignment of the offensive linemen, tight ends, and running backs to protect the quarterback on a passing play.

Blind-Side Tackle

The blind-side tackle is the tackle who protects the quarterback's back side, or "blind" side. For a right-handed quarterback, it's the tackle on the left side. For a left-handed quarterback, it's the tackle on the right side. It's an important position on the field because a quarterback who drops straight back into the pocket is susceptible to fumbling—or, more important, to injury—if he is sacked from behind by a defensive player who gets around the blind-side tackle.

The Toughest Spot on the Line

You'll often hear announcers talk about how difficult it is to play the blind-side tackle position. In some ways that's because if that tackle gets beat, it's the most noticeable. The quarterback takes a big hit, maybe there's a fumble, and everybody in the stands or watching on television points to the blind-side tackle.

But to me either tackle position can be tough to play. Whichever tackle is on the open or weak side, that is (any tackle who doesn't have a tight end there beside him). He doesn't necessarily have to be on the blind side. If there's nobody to restrict the alignment of the defensive player, he can really widen his stance or line up farther away from the offensive tackle to create an advantage. Or he can do different things from an alignment standpoint just because he's got a wide-open rush.

Pass Protection

Watch the offensive line to see how teams protect their quarterback. They can utilize a man-for-man scheme or a zone. In Dallas we zoned everything in pass protection. We didn't man anything. That's because if the defensive line tries a twist or some sort of maneuver, our offensive linemen remain on the same level, and you're still in good shape. Let's say the defender lined up over our left guard starts to move to that guard's left. Now the defender lined up over our tackle starts moving to the inside, meaning the tackle starts moving to his right toward the guard. So the guard and the tackle would bump shoulders, and they would "pass off" the game the defensive guys were running (they exchange assignments). In other words, when they bump, the guard switches to the defender coming to the inside, while the tackle goes to the player coming to the outside. It's a lot like switching on defense in basketball.

Now, if the offensive line was playing a man-for-man defense, each blocker would have to stay with his assignment. In turn the tackle would have to try to stay with his defender. You still see some offensive lines trying to play it that way, but that's very difficult to do.

History Book

It's very rare to see the football in the hands of an offensive lineman, but it happens occasionally. In 2002 the Chiefs won their season opener in large part because of the heads-up play of one of their linemen. Kansas City trailed 39–37 and apparently was down to its last play when quarterback Trent Green dropped back to pass in his own territory. Green was about to be sacked when he was spun around by a defender and lateraled the ball to guard John Tait. The alert Tait rumbled 35 yards before he was pushed out of bounds at the Browns' 30 yard line as time ran out. But there also was an unsportsmanlike penalty called on a Cleveland player—and a game cannot end with a penalty on the defense. So 15 yards were tacked on to the end of Tait's run, and Morten Andersen kicked a 33-yard field goal to give the Chiefs a wild, 40–39 victory.

A good pocket gives the quarterback good vision down the field and the ability to step into his throw. The Dallas offensive line provides Troy Aikman with the confidence to proceed through his progression without being pressured.

Photo by Ron St. Angelo

Run Blocking

Every offensive lineman likes a game plan that features lots of running. Coming hard off the line of scrimmage and initiating contact enables them to be more physical and more aggressive than in pass blocking. Sometimes defenses will try to combat that aggressiveness with stunts and twists. And the way I look at it, that's a big reason why you have a fullback as a backup. (Okay, so I'm a little biased about it!)

If a defense pulls a stunt, the offensive linemen still should be coming off the ball at 100 miles per hour. If a lineman's guy stunts and the lineman misses him, the lineman just passes the defender off to the fullback and goes on to the next level (the linebackers). Let's say the guard comes off the ball, and the defender who was on his outside shoulder stunts to the inside with a hard charge, and the guard misses him. Well, the one thing the guard simply cannot do is turn around. So he goes on to the next level and takes on the linebacker, knowing that his fullback was supposed to block the linebacker.

That's why it's important for the offensive linemen to know what all of his teammates are doing in the blocking scheme in the running game. And that's the good thing about having a fullback. Because if anybody gets beat quick and the defense penetrates the backfield, the fullback is going to be there to clean it up and give the running back a chance to get to the next defender instead of immediately getting stuffed, or tackled for a loss.

Gridiron Glossary

A **stunt** is a type of game played by defensive linemen or linebackers. Instead of just charging straight ahead and taking on their blockers, one player might loop behind another or they might cross in an attempt to confuse the blockers. See the figure on page 153.

The "Clip Zone"

Technically, it's legal to clip a player—block him in the back below the waist—when run blocking on a running play that's going between the tackles, as long as that player being blocked is not already engaged with another player. But I think that anything that jeopardizes the health or well-being of the players should be a foul. I just don't believe in the idea of a "clip zone" (clipping is not called within 3 yards of the line of scrimmage). And when you start doing things where you make contact and roll, then that's going into a whole new area.

I wouldn't even call it unethical—I would call it immoral. That's a guy's livelihood you are endangering when you dive at the back of his legs. Take Dwight Stephenson, who played for the Miami Dolphins from 1980 to 1987. I don't care what anybody says, he was the best center who ever played the game. He was dominating. And yet he gets a cheap shot that takes his knees out and he's done. You just don't do something to jeopardize another player's career.

Pursuit of the ball is one of the cornerstones of any successful defense.

Photo by Ron St. Angelo

PART FOUR

Defense

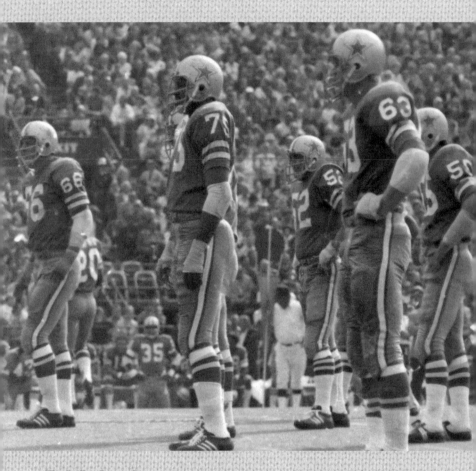

The Dallas Doomsday Defense took its place among the best units to play the game.

CHAPTER FOURTEEN

The Importance of Defense

An Admission

Defense wins championships.

There, I said it. Those words are not easy for a former offensive player to say. But I had to admit it on a telecast last season, too. Right there on the air, in front of millions of viewers—not to mention sideline reporter Tony Siragusa, a former NFL defensive lineman, who happily reminds me of it whenever he gets the chance. However, to be a champion you must have balance within your team. If your offense is not productive, it doesn't matter how good your defense is.

I think that playing offense is more fun than defense and attracts more notoriety. Playing offense provides the challenge of trying to execute the game plan that you had practiced all week long against your opponent on Sunday. But if you want to win a Super Bowl or a national championship, you have to be able to play defense. There are very few exceptions.

Moose's Memories

In high school I played defense. I played safety when I was younger, then moved to outside linebacker. Then, when I went to Syracuse, I went in there as a fullback and a linebacker. For my first three days as a freshman in college, we did drills in which everybody played offense and everybody played defense. That whole time, you wonder what they're looking for, what they're trying to see.

I would have played linebacker if that's what they wanted me to do. I felt very fortunate to be where I was, so it didn't matter to me—wherever they wanted me, I'd be there. In the end they decided I belonged at fullback.

Dictating Tempo

It used to be that defensive players did just that—they defended their team's goal. Defense was more passive than aggressive.

Oh, sure, there have always been aggressive individuals on defense. I think back to some of the great defensive players of the Pittsburgh Steelers or the Oakland Raiders who played when I was growing up. Or to the defenses in Miami and in Dallas in the seventies, too. Or even before that to some of the Hall of Famers on the Chicago Bears or the Green Bay Packers, like Dick Butkus and Ray Nitschke. And, obviously, great defenses did their own unique things.

But to me it was always about personnel. You look at Pittsburgh, and they had "Mean" Joe Greene and L. C. Greenwood on the defensive line, Jack Lambert and Jack Ham at linebacker, Mel Blount in the secondary—right on down the line, one player after another. It was just unbelievable. Same thing in Dallas. A great collection of players there, too. All those great teams played different schemes—whether it was the Steel Curtain or Doomsday and the Cowboys Flex Defense—but then on top of that, they had great players executing those schemes.

It is a relatively recent phenomenon, though, that instead of sitting

Daryl's Best

The Chicago Bears are a team to watch in the coming seasons, because of their defense. Lovie Smith is going to do just fine there. They didn't win a whole lot of games in Smith's first year as the head coach in 2004, but their defense exhibited some of the traits that Smith's defenses showed when he was the coordinator in St. Louis, and before that in Tampa Bay, where he was an assistant. And the big thing is that they have a lot of players locked into contracts until 2008 or 2009. They have a chance to have guys playing together for a long time, four or five years. That's something that really can't be underestimated on a defense. And they've already got players like linebacker Brian Urlacher and safety Mike Brown who provide the defense with a solid core to begin with. If they can ever get some stability at the quarterback position, watch out!

back and reacting to the offense, the defense is executing more aggressive pressure packages, trying to dictate tempo. The fronts and coverages are much more complicated as they actively work to force the hand of the offense. In other words, defenses are becoming more offensive.

When I say this change to a more "offensive" defense is relatively recent, I'm going back to the early to mid-1980s. This new approach started when Buddy Ryan was the defensive coordinator in Chicago. The Bears' defense under Ryan was the first one that really said, "Look, this is what we're going to do. You're going to have to figure out a way to stop us—not the other way around. We're bringing the house [blitzing more players than can be blocked], at least every once in a while. Sometimes we'll show that, but then we'll back out of it, but you're not going to know when, so you're going to have to be ready for it. We're not going to just sit here in a four-man line and play Cover 2 all day." It was very unconventional, and it forced offenses to change their blocking schemes. The Bears were the first team that I can really remember doing that.

History Book

I'll say this: Defenses sure get the good nicknames. From the "Fearsome Foursome" to the "Purple People Eaters," these names evoke images of aggressive, intimidating guys who punish opposing ballcarriers. Chicago's defense, which has had such stars as Bronko Nagurski, Dick Butkus, and Mike Singletary, has long been known as the "Monsters of the Midway" (a reference to the Midway, a city park on the south side). In the 1960s and the 1970s, the Los Angeles Rams front line was called the "Fearsome Foursome"—guys like Merlin Olsen and Deacon Jones may not have been so fearsome off the field, but they definitely were on it. Around the same time, Minnesota's defensive front was called the "Purple People Eaters." The Dolphins had the "No-Name Defense," because they didn't have a whole lot of guys who people around the country could recognize, and later the "Killer B's," because a bunch of their guys had last names that started with B. The "Steel Curtain," of course, helped Pittsburgh win four Super Bowls in the 1970s, a couple coming against the Dallas "Doomsday Defense." One year, though, the Cowboys beat Denver's "Orange Crush" defense in the Super Bowl.

Linebackers

The majority of the personnel today who are the playmakers on the defensive side of the ball are the linebackers—such as Ray Lewis in Baltimore or Brian Urlacher in Chicago.

The linebackers are the most athletic players on the defensive side of the ball. They must be able to take on fullbacks and offensive linemen to stop the running game and to cover tight ends, running backs, and at times wide receivers in pass defense. Depending on the defensive personnel, there will be either three linebackers (4-3 defense) or four linebackers (3-4 defense) (see figures on pages 134 and 135). In a 4-3 defense there is a strong-side outside linebacker who lines up on the same side as the tight end, a weakside outside linebacker who lines up on the opposite side as the tight end, and a middle linebacker. In a 3-4 defense there are two linebackers to each side. There is a strong-side inside and strong-side outside linebacker and a weakside inside and weakside outside linebacker. Some 3-4 defenses are based on a right and left principle. The inside and outside linebackers will play on the right and left and not change in accordance to the tight end.

Linebackers generally are the surest tacklers on the team, and they're usually the guys who spend more hours in the film room than anyone else, too. Some of them are almost coaches on the field. Teammates look to linebackers for leadership, and opponents plan ways to keep them from being too disruptive. The opposition may even change their blocking scheme to ensure that a linebacker such as Baltimore's Ray Lewis doesn't make a game-changing play.

As offenses have become more and more sophisticated, coaches have asked more and more of their linebackers. Ever since the days of Sam Huff and Ray Nitschke and Dick Butkus, linebackers have had a reputation as intimidating, hard-hitting defenders capable of delivering a momentum-changing blow to an opposing ballcarrier or quarterback. But now, more often than not, linebackers are asked not only to defend the run and rush the passer, but also to drop back into zone pass defense or cover running backs or tight ends man for man on pass patterns. So they not only have to be big and strong, but they must also be athletic and quick.

Such versatility is a key trait. A guy like Ray Lewis, for instance, is too quick off the ball and too athletic for a lot of the big offensive linemen who try to block him. So a lot of times, he doesn't even have to take on the block. He'll just go around it. He doesn't have to take the punishment every time, so why should he? On the flip side, when he gets a smaller, quicker back who tries to block him, he doesn't have to rely on his quickness. Now he can use his strength.

Sometimes, when you're watching a game, you might see a linebacker calling out things before a play or pointing across the line of scrimmage. He may be telling his teammates about something he recognizes from the formation or pointing to an offset back or an extra wide receiver. Often middle linebackers are big film guys who know when they see certain packages, like if the offense comes out with three wide receivers or is in a certain set, that a pass play is coming. Or he may recognize tendencies simply from how a guy lines up.

History Book

When I first joined the Cowboys in 1989, Lawrence Taylor had already been in the league for almost a decade. But while I missed his most dominant seasons, he was still one of those players whose whereabouts on the field you wanted to know at all times.

From the time the New York Giants drafted him out of North Carolina in 1981, it was obvious that "LT," as he was called, usually was the best player on the field in a given game. And it was Taylor who is most often credited with revolutionizing the linebacker position. Up until then, linebackers most often played "read and react"—process what's happening on a play and then respond accordingly. But Taylor didn't want to wait and see what was going to happen; he wanted to make something happen. He was a defensive star whose style of play could take over a game.

Defensive Linemen

Next to the linebackers, it's the pass rushers on the defensive line—defensive ends such as Jevon Kearse in Philadelphia, Simeon Rice in Tampa Bay, and Leonard Little in St. Louis—who are the big play-makers that garner the most attention.

Like the offensive line, the setup of the defensive line is dependent on its personnel. A 4-3 defense will have an end and tackle on each side. Some philosophies will align their defensive tackles based on strength, according to where the tight end is, and others will simply play it based on a right and left principle. The tackles will align from the outside shoulder of the right guard to the outside shoulder of the left guard and anywhere in between. Defensive ends generally play according to a right and left principle. By game plan some speed-rush defensive ends will align to the open tackle (tackle without a tight end lined up next to him). The ends will align from the inside shoulder of the offensive tackle to the outside shoulder of the tight end (if it is the open side, to the outside shoulder of the offensive tackle or, with coaches' permission, a little wider). In a 4-3 defense the main job of the defensive end is to pressure the quarter-back, and tackles in the run game are a plus. Stopping the run is the responsibility of the defensive tackles and linebackers.

The 3-4 defense has a defensive end on each side and a nose tackle, or noseguard, who typically lines up on the center. The defensive ends in a 3-4 defense are usually bigger than defensive ends in a 4-3 defense. Their main job is to stop the run, and any pressure they generate in the passing game is a bonus. The linebackers are the pass rush specialists in the 3-4. And then there is the noseguard. He is the anchor of the 3-4 defense, and if you want to be a good 3-4 defense, you better have a good nose tackle. It is one of the most difficult and thankless—except from your teammates— jobs in the NFL.

Obviously, the best defensive ends are those who can stop the run and rush the passer. Leonard Little is such a player. But what every-body wants on the defensive side of the ball is the pass rusher who

Gridiron Glossary

Nose Tackle

In a 3-4 alignment (three down linemen and four linebackers), the nose tackle—or, sometimes, the noseguard—is the defensive tackle who lines up over the center. In a 4-3 alignment (four down linemen and three linebackers), teams utilize two defensive tackles who generally line up opposite the guards on the offensive line. But they can also line up over the center.

You might notice more and more teams today rotating their defensive linemen during the course of a game or even a series. The Falcons like to do that and bring in someone like defensive tackle Travis Hall. That can make it really tough on an offensive lineman. He's constantly got a fresh set of legs coming at him in passing situations.

the offense always has to account for—the guy the offensive players see on film and say, "If we don't find a way to block him, then our chances of winning are not very good." When I was playing, Reggie White (who was with the Eagles in the late 1980s and early 1990s when I was in Dallas, then later went to Green Bay, a team we met in the playoffs several times) was that guy. You just simply could not let him get on a roll.

There are some excellent pass-rushing defensive tackles, too, players who really can make a push toward the quarterback. When I was in Dallas, Minnesota's John Randle was one of the best, and Warren Sapp was dominant for years in Tampa Bay. Other schemes ask the interior defensive linemen to occupy the blockers up front and allow the linebackers to get to the ballcarrier or the ends to reach the quarterback.

Moose's Memories

The bad thing about playing Philadelphia in the early 1990s was more than just Reggie White. We knew we always had to account for Reggie. Well, the Eagles also had Jerome Brown and Clyde Simmons and Andy Harmon on their defensive line. What do you do? And then they had that 46 defense—I mean, my goodness!

Defensive Backs

The defensive backs are the cornerbacks and the safeties. Also collectively known as the secondary, they represent the last line of defense.

The two cornerbacks are the defenders who line up on the outside and are close to the line of scrimmage. Cornerbacks almost always line up on the same side of the field, either you play right cornerback or left cornerback. However, some defensive coordinators will match the opposition's best wide receiver if he has a special cornerback, oftentimes referred to as a "shut down corner." Deion Sanders is probably the last legitimate shut down corner. He and Michael Irvin had some epic battles when Deion played for the Falcons and 49ers.

There are also two safeties. These are the defenders lined up deep in the secondary, the last line of defense. Their alignments will be dictated by the offense's strength of formation (where the tight end lines up). The strong safety will line up on the same side as the tight end. He is usually more physical than his counterpart, the free safety, and at times will be aligned on the linebacker level to help stop the run game. The free safety is usually a better cover guy than the strong safety and has a nose for the ball.

You'll often hear announcers talk about how defensive backs need to have a short memory. Well, what they mean is that every defensive back is going to get beat occasionally—and when a defensive back gets beat, it invariably means a big play for the offense, often a deep pass or even a touchdown. It's also often apparent to the fans in the stands and the audience watching on television what player was beaten on the long pass play, or who didn't get over in time to help out on the coverage. If a defensive lineman misses a play, the linebackers at the next level can help out. If a linebacker misses a play, the defensive backs at the next level can help out. But if a defensive back misses a play, there is no next level.

The best defensive backs don't play with any fear, though. They forget about any past transgressions and move on to the next play. In fact they tend to want the ball thrown in their direction. Cornerback Deion Sanders was one who always wanted the ball to come his way. He even used to bait opposing quarterbacks by playing off his man just enough so that the quarterback thought he could get the ball to the receiver—but not too far that his great closing speed couldn't bring him back to bat the ball away or, often, create an interception. Deion is such an amazing athlete that he played for Baltimore in 2004 even though he had been out of football for three full seasons. That year, he returned an interception for a touchdown for the ninth time in his career—only Rod Woodson has done it more times.

Some safeties, like Brian Dawkins in Philadelphia and Roy Williams in Dallas, are the defenders that a team asks to be its big-play guys on that side of the ball. A defense has to take advantage of the strength of its personnel. If a team has someone as good as Roy Williams, it wants to utilize him as much as possible.

Daryl's Best

A couple of guys in Baltimore would get a whole lot more notice all around the league if it wasn't for middle linebacker Ray Lewis, who is so dominant that he gets most of the headlines. One of those guys is another linebacker, Edgerton Hartwell. He is such a good player and does his job so well at inside linebacker that I've always said if he played anywhere else but alongside Lewis in Baltimore, everybody would know him. Now we'll find out because he signed with the Atlanta Falcons and won't be playing in Ray's shadow any more.

Another is safety Ed Reed. He sometimes gets lost in the shuffle because of Ray, but he is a real playmaker. Look for the ball when the Ravens' opponent has possession, and you'll probably find Ed close by. Of course, the secret about Ed is out now—he blew his cover by winning the league's defensive player of the year award last season.

Buddy Ryan, who was the architect of the 46 Defense for the Chicago Bears, was paid the ultimate compliment when his players carried him off the field on their shoulders after Chicago beat New England in Super Bowl XX.

Photo courtesy of Chicago Bears Football Club

CHAPTER FIFTEEN

Base Defenses

3-4 or 4-3?

Every team carries a base defense. They have to have one. But how much do you see it anymore? Not as much as you used to. It used to be that teams would stay in their base defense probably 75 to 80 percent of the time, or even more. Nowadays, maybe it's 50 to 55 percent of the time.

Most teams use their base defense on first down. Then, once they get past first down, the defensive call is based on situations—second and medium (4 to 6 yards), short (3 or fewer yards), or long (7+ yards) will have different defenses, and third and medium, short, or long will have different defenses. And what the offense does personnel-wise, the defense often will react to. Watch to see if the offense brings in a third wide receiver. Does the defense bring in a nickel back to match, or does it decide to remain in its base defense?

Whether a team lines up in a 3-4 (three down linemen and four linebackers) or a 4-3 (four down linemen and three linebackers) as a base defense really is just a matter of preference for the head coach and defensive coordinator, combined with the personnel a club has.

What's the Difference?

A lot of people will tell you the only difference between the 3-4 and 4-3 is taking a linebacker and putting him in a three-point stance at the end position on the line of scrimmage. And from an offensive perspective, I can tell you that it's not really a big deal whether you're facing a 3-4 or a 4-3. You have covered it all week long in preparation of the game plan. When we played a 4-3 team, our blocking assignments were the same for all 4-3 teams. They changed slightly versus a 3-4 but were the same for all 3-4 defenses.

The key is that a defense has to have the talent to play whichever alignment it decides to go with. A team with more quality linebackers than defensive linemen is going to be better off in a 3-4, for instance. Often you see defensive coaches who have one scheme or the other that they've run their whole careers, and they come in and try to fit the players to the scheme—it's a square-peg, round-hole type of situation. But the best coaches come in, take a look around at the personnel they have, and make the scheme fit the players. Maybe they tweak their system a little bit to maximize the abilities of the players they have.

That's what the Baltimore Ravens did in 2000. Number one, they had a lot of guys who had been playing together for four or five years. But number two, they had great athletes in a great system taught by a great teacher (defensive coordinator Marvin Lewis). Every player knew what his teammates were going to do, and they executed well. You talk to people who played against Baltimore that year, and they

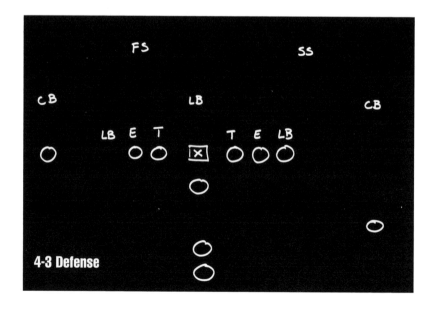

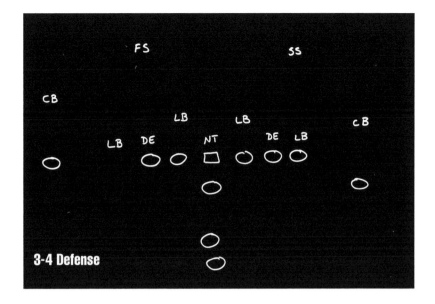

3-4 Defense

say they knew what the Ravens were going to do on defense in almost every situation—they rarely did anything different. They were just so good at what they did, and they did not make any mistakes.

The 46 Defense

The 46 defense began in Chicago in the early to mid-1980s, when Buddy Ryan was the defensive coordinator for head coach Mike Ditka. In the Bears' 46 they lined up four linemen, four linebackers, and three defensive backs, although one of those linebackers was more of a hybrid linebacker and defensive back who positioned himself near the line of scrimmage. The Bears won Super Bowl XX when the defense was at the height of its effectiveness, and Ryan soon was off to Philadelphia to become its head coach. His defensive coordinator was a former Bears defensive back, Jeff Fisher, who eventually moved on to Tennessee to become the head coach there.

That coaching lineage helped spread the 46 to different parts of the league. And just like any other effective scheme in pro football, imitation is the sincerest form of flattery. Bits and pieces of the 46 are still utilized by teams throughout the NFL.

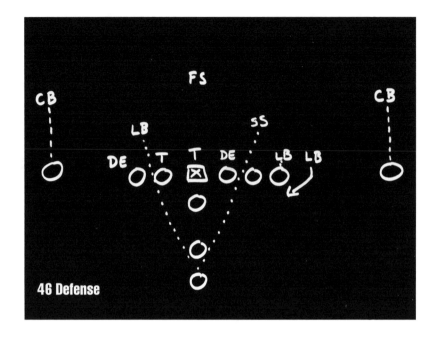

46 Defense

From my perspective the 46 forced an offense to change its normal style of play. Some things you just couldn't do because at times they would rush more defenders than you could block. It gets back to the defense dictating tempo to the offense. There were times when the Bears—and, later, the Eagles when Ryan became the head coach in Philadelphia—would blitz seven or eight players. It was very unconventional, and it changed a lot of the blocking schemes.

What the Bears' defense did was to isolate every offensive lineman in one-on-one situations so there was no way for anyone on the line to help anyone else out. And then, when the offense lined up and saw the people Chicago had—Dan Hampton, Richard Dent, Otis Wilson, all those good players across the front—knowing that no help was coming, well, that made it very difficult for them.

The Eagles did that a little bit, too, when Buddy went to Philadelphia. They kept defensive end Reggie White on the outside in certain alignments, but then they would move White inside over the center or wherever they felt he could get the best matchup and where there were no uncovered offensive linemen who could help his man.

There were just so many things that could come out of that exact same look. Offenses just didn't know what the 46 was going to do. And that gets back to the point we made earlier: Defenses began trying to get the upper hand by becoming more offensive in their approach.

Beating the 46

There are a few ways to attack the 46 Defense. In 1985, when the Dolphins handed Chicago its only defeat of the season—they beat the Bears 38–24 in a memorable Monday night game after Chicago had opened the season with twelve consecutive victories—the number one reason was quarterback Dan Marino. His quick release made the short passing game work, and it didn't allow the Bears pass rushers to get to him before the ball came out. It also helped that the Dolphins had Dwight Stephenson on the offensive line. Stephenson was perhaps the best center in NFL history and always was better than anyone he lined up against.

The 46 was so new and different that it took offenses a while to catch on to it. But everybody, I'm sure, watched what Miami did on that Monday night. They learned that you've still got to be able to run the ball, especially to the weak side—that's probably one of the

History Book

Unlike a lot of notable defensive schemes, the name "46 defense" has nothing to do with how the players align. Instead, 46 was the uniform number of Doug Plank, a safety who played for the Bears from 1975 to 1982. Plank was a favorite of defensive coordinator Buddy Ryan for his aggressiveness and hard hitting, and Ryan named the defense after him. Ironically, Plank wasn't playing anymore when the 46 helped carry Chicago to the Super Bowl in the 1985 season.

most important things from the standpoint of an offensive scheme—
and that you've got to be able to get the ball out of the quarterback's
hand quickly.

But mostly, it comes down to personnel. An offense needs to have
a strong center and good linemen without a weak link across the
board, and defenses need to have the players up front and strong cornerbacks who can play on the outside without a lot of help.

The 46 as a Base

Most teams still carry a little bit of the 46 today. If nothing else,
they'll slip it in during a few games just so offenses have to watch it
on tape. That way their opponents have to worry about it and spend
time preparing for it. But most defenses know they don't have the
personnel to run it all the time. It's one of those things that, sure, it
looks great when it's done right, but how many people can do it
right?

The Titans, of course, still run the 46 some with Jeff Fisher as
their head coach. Occasionally, the Baltimore Ravens have had it in
their package. The Washington Redskins and New York Giants have
always had a little of it, too. John Fox, who was the Giants' defensive
coordinator before he became the head coach of the Carolina
Panthers, carries it. But you don't get a heavy dose of the 46 like you
did with the Bears. That was Chicago's base defense in the mid-1980s.
Today it's more of a supplemental front for teams that utilize it.

Communication

Whatever defense a team utilizes, the key factor is communication—
making sure all eleven players are on the same page. That's one of
the things that has made the Baltimore Ravens' defense so good
recently—especially when the team won the Super Bowl in 2000.
They had guys at each level who could communicate with each other
and with the other players at their positions. At every level someone
was in charge of relaying messages back and forth. All of a sudden,

before the ball is snapped, that information is transferred to all eleven guys.

Up front the Ravens had defensive end Michael McCrary, in the middle they had linebacker Ray Lewis, and in the secondary they had safety Rod Woodson. Those three were always communicating back and forth and passing things on so that everyone on the defense knew exactly what was going on.

The Dallas defense tackles Robert Smith of the Minnesota Vikings. A good running back can make a few guys miss tackles, but not this many.

Photo by Ron St. Angelo

Run Defense

Who Makes the Tackles?

With all the rule changes making it easier to throw the ball in the NFL, the passing game is becoming a bigger and bigger part of most teams' game plans. However, I still think that stopping the run is the number one objective of any defense. There is nothing fancy about run defense. It's an attitude. It's about being physical and defeating your man.

The key thing in run defense is getting to the ball. Sounds simple, right? But when a defense goes up against an explosive running back such as Kansas City's Priest Holmes or Seattle's Shaun Alexander, or a quarterback who can hurt you with his running ability, such as Atlanta's Michael Vick or Philadelphia's Donovan McNabb, everybody needs to go to the ball. Otherwise, once a ballcarrier breaks through one level, there's nobody there in support—and that's when big runs happen.

Who makes the tackles depends in large part on a team's philosophy and system, but also on who they have on their team. In Baltimore, for instance, middle linebacker Ray Lewis is supposed to make the tackles. In Chicago, linebacker Brian Urlacher is supposed to make the tackles. These guys are supposed to be the playmakers. Some of the other defensive philosophies around the league will allow the down linemen a little more leeway in what they're doing. Their job is not to just occupy blockers so the linebackers can run free and make tackles. If they can get upfield and make a play, do it.

Some teams only ask their defensive linemen to prevent offensive players from getting to the second level and blocking their linebackers. They'll just have the defensive linemen grab the offensive linemen to keep them from getting to their linebackers (which is why they call that holding now). The defensive linemen are just there to occupy the blockers. Former Tampa Bay (and current Oakland Raiders) defensive tackle Warren Sapp used to do a good job getting an outside shade, a position almost between the tackle and the guard, just to disrupt the blocking scheme. Defensive tackle Chris Hovan in Minnesota is another guy who was really effective at that.

Run Support

We learned something from Tampa Bay defensive coordinator Monte Kiffin last year that is interesting—and innovative. It's a way of getting the safety involved in run support. That's a way of bringing the safety down from his normal alignment in the secondary to the linebacker level to help stop the running game. Whether the safety can help in run support depends on what defense a team is in. In Cover 2 the safeties are going to be deep, so the strong safety won't be able to help against the run. But if the defense brings eight men in the box, the strong safety drops back in near the line of scrimmage and everybody plays a gap defense.

Here's how it works: Every defender has a gap (an area between offensive linemen)—A, B, C, and D on one side of the line and A, B, C, and D on the other side—he is responsible for filling at the snap of the ball. I truly believe that the ball always finds its way to an opening, whether it is where the play is designed to go or where a defender didn't fill his gap. But what Monte Kiffin's defense tries to do is have that safety fill the gap that comes open and get there at the same time as the ball.

So the running back takes the handoff, and a gap comes open. He sees the opening and tries to get to it, but the safety has timed it to meet the running back in that area and stop the play. In theory, if everybody does his job, there will be no running lane. It sounds great, but don't forget the offensive players get paid too. If even one defender doesn't do his job, there will be a running lane for the running back.

Eight Is Enough

If there are eight men in the box, sure, offenses can always try to throw over them. But I've always felt that an offense has to try to run the football no matter what. If you're a good team, you have to be able to run the ball against any defense, even an eight-man front. Sometimes it's just a matter of the running back making a play. You know, the offense can account for seven guys blocked, so the eighth guy is up to him. He has to make the defender miss the tackle. That's where a lot of long runs come in, especially against the blitz. A running back makes a guy miss and pops through that first tier, then it's 10 or 12 yards before he comes to the next level. Also, offenses can adjust their blocking schemes at the line of scrimmage to allow the farthest defender from the point of attack to be the unblocked man.

Just because there are eight men up front doesn't necessarily mean

Gridiron Glossary

The Box

There's no official "box," it's just the imaginary area near the line of scrimmage in which most of the defenders line up at the beginning of a play. A normal base defense will include seven players in the box: either four down linemen and three linebackers, or three down linemen and four linebackers. When an announcer says that a defense has put eight men in the box, it's usually one of the safeties who is the extra man. When you get that extra guy in there, it makes it all the tougher for a running back to find a place to go.

they are going to bring eight—maybe they'll only rush six or seven—but the offense doesn't know how many rushers are coming or from where they are coming.

Still, some teams have audibles just based on the number of defenders in the box. A quarterback has a run play called, but if he sees the defense has brought an eighth man in the box, he automatically audibles to a pass. Or he comes to the line and yells, "Opposite"—meaning it might be the exact same play but run to the other side.

Change of Pace

You might watch the Falcons play and see Warrick Dunn running up and down the field, and then notice T. J. Duckett is in the backfield on the next series of plays. Why? If Warrick Dunn is so effective, why take him out of the game at all? Because it presents a difficult situation for a run defense when an offense brings in that change-of-pace running back. It's a real big changeup to have a shifty, elusive runner in for one set of plays and then come back with a powerful inside runner on the next set.

The defense always has to be aware of who is in the game and what each back's strengths and weaknesses are. In Atlanta head coach

History Book

One of the more dramatic change-of-pace backfields in recent memory was in New York a few years ago, where the Giants utilized Tiki Barber and Ron Dayne. The bigger Dayne was called "Thunder" and the smaller, faster Barber was called "Lightning." It worked pretty well for a while, like when Barber ran for more than 1,000 yards and 8 touchdowns and Dayne added 770 yards and 5 touchdowns in 2000. Unfortunately for Giants' fans, Thunder and Lightning fizzled out pretty quick after that when Dayne just wasn't scoring enough points or running for enough yardage.

Jim Mora likes to get Duckett into the game early on, maybe by the third series (the third time the offense takes the field). It not only creates a big changeup for the defense, but it also gives the starter, Warrick Dunn, a rest. Warrick isn't a big guy, and this way he doesn't have to take a pounding all game long for 25 or 30 carries. It keeps him fresh, not only for the fourth quarter of a game but also for late in the season.

If you can't get to the quarterback, get your hands up. Dallas' Greg Ellis and Dat Nguyen make things difficult for the Detroit Lions Joey Harrington.

Photo by Ron St. Angelo

CHAPTER SEVENTEEN

Pass Defense

Putting on the Pressure

The goal of the pass defense is to stop the opponent's passing game. The defense uses a combination of the pass rush (a normal rush of four guys or a blitz of five or more) and pass coverage, which can be zone, man, or a combination.

One of the most important things for any NFL pass defense is to be able to generate pressure on the opposing quarterback and make him feel uncomfortable. Almost everybody would agree to that. But, like just about anything else in football, different coaches have different ways of looking at the means to that end.

Jim Mora Jr., for instance, when he was the defensive coordinator in San Francisco and now as head coach in Atlanta, wants to come after the quarterback with a lot of different pressure packages, including the zone blitz. Maybe he'll bring an extra linebacker up inside to apply pressure or bring a defensive back off the corner. He wants to give the quarterback a bunch of different looks and a bunch of different things to think about, and he wants to try to confuse him and prevent him from feeling comfortable.

On the flip side there's a team like Seattle. Ray Rhodes, the defensive coordinator there, is a lot more conservative with his blitz packages. He has more basic packages and asks his players to execute them perfectly. A team that can generate enough pressure on the quarterback with its four down linemen doesn't have to blitz a whole lot. And if you can do that, it's going to be very difficult for any quarterback to be effective in the passing game. If you can generate pres-

Rules to Know

Defensive Holding

Quite a big deal was made about stricter enforcement of the defensive holding rule in 2004. A defensive back is allowed to bump a wide receiver within 5 yards of the line of scrimmage. But he cannot tug on or grab the wide receiver's jersey at any time. And the defender is not allowed to make any contact outside of 5 yards that might impede or alter the route of the pass catcher. Only "incidental" contact is permitted.

sure with your four defensive linemen, you can play coverage with your remaining seven defenders. It will be tough to find open throwing lanes in that situation.

Cover 2

You almost can't watch a football telecast these days without hearing some announcer refer to Cover 2. In layman's terms Cover 2 is just two deep safeties. The safeties are the two deepest defenders in the defensive secondary. The strong safety usually lines up on the side of the field where the tight end is lined up, and the free safety will be on the other half of the field. Safeties are the last line of defense, but it has become commonplace to see them lined up close to the line of scrimmage involved in the defense's pressure package. In Cover 2 each of the safeties is responsible for defending his side of the field—one safety has one half of the field and the other safety has the other half. Nothing can get beyond them.

Out of that, teams can do various things, like Cover 2 Man. Teams will play man-for-man coverage underneath (on shorter routes) with their linebackers and cornerbacks, with the safeties still deep in Cover 2. But most of the time, Cover 2 means the defense has two safeties deep with five defenders in front of them, each responsible for his specific zone.

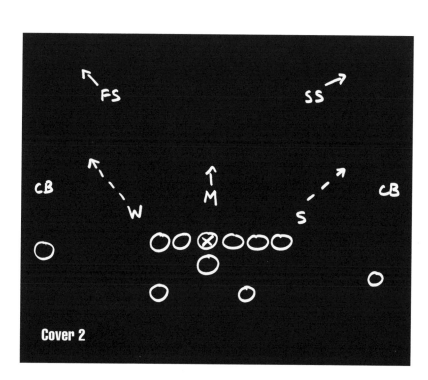

Cover 2

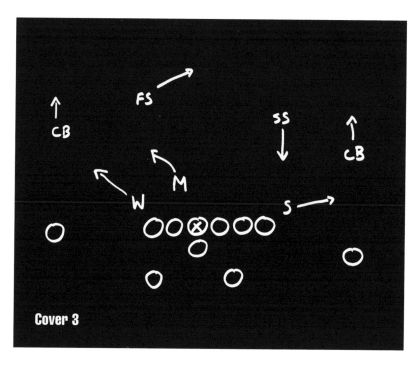

Cover 3

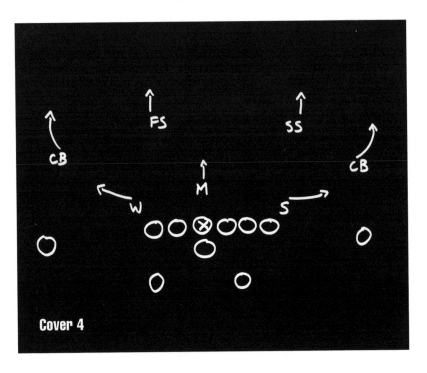

Cover 4

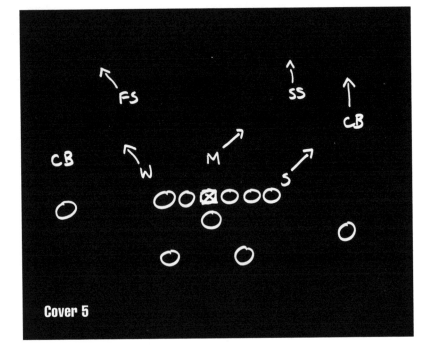

Cover 5

Gridiron Glossary

Pass coverage is a scheme or philosophy to defend against a passing play. It could be man-to-man coverage, zone coverage, or a combination of the two. Any defensive player could be involved in pass coverage, even a defensive lineman in a zone blitz scheme.

By extension, then, teams also can come out in Cover 3, with three defensive backs deep, or even Cover 4, with four defensive backs fanned deep across the width of the field.

Umbrella Defense

One of the early versions of the Cover 2 was the Umbrella Defense that the New York Giants devised in 1950. The Cleveland Browns had just entered the NFL after four years of dominating play in the All-America Football Conference, and they brought along quarterback Otto Graham and a powerful passing attack. Coach Steve Owen and defensive back Tom Landry, the future Cowboys coach, came up with a system whereby the defensive backs fanned into sort of a dome shape (hence, the name "Umbrella Defense"), and the defensive ends had the option of dropping back into pass coverage. Those defensive ends eventually developed into today's outside linebacker, so the Umbrella also was a precursor to today's 4-3 base defense.

The Tampa 2

Cover 2 has been around forever—probably some form of it almost from the time they began throwing the football. But the Buccaneers did it a little bit differently in Tampa Bay beginning in the 1990s: They had the inside linebacker turn and run with the number two receiver to the strongside when they had Hardy Nickerson there.

Daryl's Best

You've got to have the cornerbacks to play Tampa 2. Pro Bowl corner-back Ronde Barber is a perfect fit there. A guy like Antoine Winfield in Minnesota would be a good fit. These are players who are good cover guys, so when teams want to drop that safety into the box, they can stick with the receivers. But also when the offense runs the ball, they aren't afraid to come up and make tackles in run support.

Nickerson was a gifted linebacker who was tough enough and strong enough to stop the run but still athletic enough to stay with receivers in pass coverage. That inside receiver generally was the tight end, so when you would see the tight end shoot down the middle of the field, you'd see Hardy Nickerson right there with him. The rest of the defense was still in Cover 2, but with that middle linebacker running the receiver down the field, it almost made it a three-deep coverage. That's why everybody started calling it the Tampa 2—it was essentially Cover 2, but there were some subtleties that Tony Dungy, then the coach of the Buccaneers, put in.

One reason that Tampa Bay became so proficient at what it did was because the Buccaneers knew that there were only certain route combinations that could be run against them because of how their pass coverage was designed. So then they saw those same routes from almost every team on a regular basis. It was a cycle: They were seeing the same routes over and over again and getting better and better at defending against them.

Games People Play

Defensive linemen can run various types of stunts in an effort to confuse the offensive line and get to the quarterback. The first thing both defenders want to do is start going forward so the offensive guard and the offensive tackle think it's a straight pass rush and not a stunt. The defensive tackle goes upfield, then creates something like a pick in basketball. He starts outside and the guard has to move with him because he has to respect his outside move. But what the defensive tackle is really trying to do is get to the inside arm of the offensive

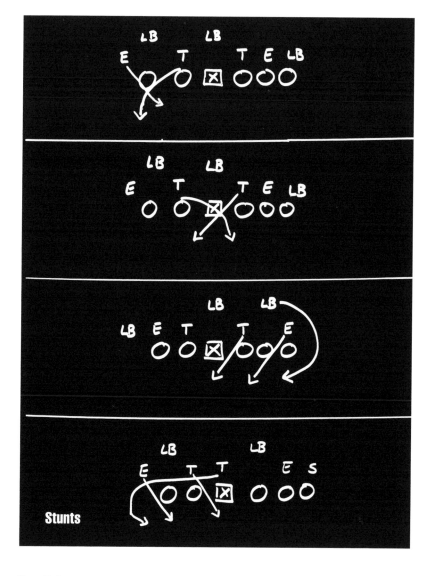

Stunts

Daryl's Best

A quick first step is one of the biggest attributes a good pass-rushing defensive end has. The Rams Leonard Little has one of the best. We did one telecast last year when the quarterback had a three-step drop, and the blockers just tried to cut him down at the line of scrimmage. Leonard just used his athletic ability and his quickness to step past the blocker and still chase down the quarterback. A lot of people around the NFL talk about the Eagles Jevon Kearse, and there's no doubt he's one of the best pass rushers out there, too. But I'd like to see some sort of a competition between Leonard and Jevon to see who can get off the line of scrimmage the fastest.

tackle so he can't pass the game back to the guard. Then the defensive end comes underneath, beats the guard, and gets to the quarterback.

In another stunt the defensive end and the defensive tackle both crash to the inside, and the defensive tackle on the other side loops all the way around to the outside to the open spot. But remember, these types of stunts take so long to complete that when the quarterback drops back only three steps, it's just not worth it. Unless the stunt is executed perfectly, there's just not enough time to get to the quarterback before the ball has already come out.

The Prevent Defense

The prevent defense prevents nothing, except possibly a victory. I am just not a big fan of it. If a team has played a particular defense the whole game—and built a lead using it—then I say stick with it. Even if it's just for one drive near the end of the game, stay in that defense.

The philosophy is that a defense doesn't want the offense to go all the way downfield in one chunk. Well, as an offensive player, I would

Gridiron Glossary

A **prevent defense** is designed to protect a lead late in a game by forcing the offense to accept smaller chunks of yardage underneath (or in front of) deep coverage instead of getting a big gain or a long touchdown by throwing over the coverage. So teams in a prevent defense will rush only four men—or even three—and have seven or eight players deep in pass coverage. The theory, of course, is that an offense that has to accept shorter completions in front of the coverage will chew up too much time, and the clock will run out before they can score enough points to make up for a deficit.

rather the opposing team get it all in one chunk and let us get back out there on the field, rather than have them complete a bunch of underneath (short) stuff, keep running out of bounds, and then kick a field goal or score a touchdown with 5 seconds left. Then it's too late and there's no time for the offense to get back on the field. Defenses need to find that common ground, when they are not in a prevent, but they're not overly aggressive up front—instead, they're playing something that is going to challenge the offense.

If I'm the defensive coordinator, here's what I'm thinking: I stay with the defense I've been in the whole game. That defense obviously has gotten me a lead so far, and I feel very comfortable doing what has already worked for me. And I've watched the other team on film, too, so I know what plays they are going to run in their two-minute drill. Sure, there might be a wrinkle or two here and there, but generally they're going to run the same plays. So, if we play this defense, then we really take that option away from them, and if we play this grouping, then we really match up well with their personnel. And I know from game preparation and from what they've run today that they're going to call certain plays on third and long. And since we're essentially in a third-and-long situation on every play now, I can still use the same defense that I used in the second quarter or in the third quarter that was successful on third and long.

Spying the Quarterback

A lot of times when defenses face a particularly mobile quarterback—say, Atlanta's Michael Vick or Minnesota's Daunte Culpepper in today's game or San Francisco's Steve Young or Philadelphia's Randall Cunningham in the past—they will utilize one player to "spy" the quarterback. Wherever the quarterback goes, the defensive guy mirrors him. The quarterback moves left, the defensive player moves right; the quarterback moves right, the defensive player moves left. Usually, it's an athletic linebacker who is assigned the task of spying, though sometimes it can be a safety or athletic defensive tackle or defensive end.

But spying is a waste of time as far as I'm concerned. First of all, a team is taking one of its players out of the regular defense for an entire play—and it may not even turn out to be necessary. And second, some of the quarterbacks they're trying to spy are among the best athletes on field. Who does a team have that is fast enough to run with Michael Vick? Who do they put on him? And even if they do have someone who is fast enough, do they have someone who is also big enough to tackle a guy such as Daunte Culpepper, who is as big as a linebacker?

A defender has to be athletic enough to run with the quarterback and big enough to make the tackle. And if a defense has someone who is that good, it plays right into the offense's hands to limit what you are asking him to do on the field.

So the solution is not spying, it's to pressure the quarterback in the pocket. Make him hurry his throws and make him uncomfortable back there. Mix and match coverages on defense, too. You don't want to play a lot of man coverage because you don't want defenders running downfield with their backs to the quarterback, so that he can take off and run. And there are little things you can do on defense, too. For instance, some people say never to let the Eagles' Donovan McNabb escape to his right because he's most dangerous there. So you tell your left defensive end to stay at home—don't get too far upfield and don't get blocked out of the play. Once he gets beyond the quarterback in the pocket, he is out of the play.

Dallas special-teams coach Joe Avezzano goes over some last-second instructions before the kickoff return team takes the field. Emmitt Smith is listening in, but you won't catch him playing special teams.

Photo by Ron St. Angelo

PART FIVE

Special
Teams

The objective of special teams is to score points. It could be on a punt or kickoff return or a PAT (point after touchdown) or field goal. Here, Cowboys kicker Billy Cundriff tries to get three points for Dallas.

Photo by Ron St. Angelo

CHAPTER EIGHTEEN

A Unique Phase

Special Teams

We've all heard talk about how important special teams are to the outcome of a football game. When the special teams are on the field, it's the phase of the game with the most potential for a big play, and at no other point in the game is there that much yardage being traded off. But here's another way to look at it: Only on special teams is the object to score every time you touch the ball. You can argue that offenses can say that, too, but often teams are just trying to set things up on offense. Maybe they're trying to maneuver into field-goal range, or put themselves in a second-and-short situation, or convert a third and 5. Or maybe they're even trying to sit on the ball and run out the clock. But on special teams, whether it's a team kicking an extra point or a field goal, or a team trying to return a punt or a kickoff, the sole objective is to score—every time. It's a unique phase of the game, and it takes a unique individual to play it.

Gridiron Glossary

The **special teams** are made up of eleven offensive and defensive players who are used in all phases of the kicking game: kickoffs, punts, extra points, and field goals.

A Special Player

I don't know if you meet someone and know he's going to be a great special-teams player, but these positions definitely take a different mentality. For one thing the most violent collisions in football, without a doubt, take place on special teams.

At some point in time, I played on every one of the special teams in Dallas. When you're older and you're in the starting lineup, that's a hard thing to do. But when you're young and you're trying to get noticed, you're trying to find your way around and understand the game, to learn the speed of the game, it's beneficial to play on special teams. A lot of players in the NFL get their start on special teams. Some just naturally pick it up coming out of college and do well.

On the other hand, it's not an automatic that just the first- and second-year players go on special teams. I know that some NFL teams, concerned about injuries to their regulars, like to use reserves or backup players, but different teams approach it differently.

The majority of your special-teams players are defensive backs, linebackers, fullbacks, or tight ends. There are some running backs out there who do a good job on special teams, too. And sometimes you'll see an offensive lineman on the wedge on kickoff returns, or an athletic defensive lineman covering kicks. Some jobs are specific to certain positions, but for the most part, it's your linebacker, defensive back, or fullback-type player out there with the special teams.

Moose's Memories

In Dallas the players on special teams were often put there because they were the best for that position regardless of whether they were starters in the regular offense or defense. Sometimes a defensive guy might go up to Joe Avezzano (our special-teams coach) before a punt or a kickoff and tell him, "Hey, Joe, I need a break. I really need a breather here." So Joe would say, "Sure, no problem. I'll tell Coach to take you out of the nickel package." He was not going to let you get out of playing on special teams. That was his philosophy.

The onside kick is one of the many unique plays that occur in the special teams phase of the game of football. Bill Bates (40) and I (48) are the designated blockers so Jay Novacek (84) can recover the kick.

Photo by Ann Johnston

Momentum Swings

It's on special teams that you have some of the biggest shifts in momentum during a game. A big hit on a kickoff return, of course, or a crushing block on a punt return—a lot of times you'll see a player clean the clock of an opponent—those are definitely momentum swings. But it can also be a punt that gets downed near the goal line, or a great tackle in kick coverage. Even a field goal, say, into the wind where you're right on the cusp of whether your kicker can make it or not. A team can really get a lift from just one play in the kicking game or from the kick-return or kick-coverage units.

Part of the Plan

More and more coaches today talk about winning the field-position battle being a big part of what they're trying to accomplish on Sunday. When they're saying things like that, they're talking mainly about special teams. Coaches place a much bigger emphasis on special teams now than even five, ten years ago. They use lots of statistics to support their cause—like percentage of drives that result in points when you start inside your own 10 yard line, inside the 20, from the 20 to the 35, the 35 to the 50, or at such and such a point, whether after a kickoff or a punt. So special teams are becoming much more of a big deal. You'll see coaches make decisions based on the field position that they can generate through the kicking game.

Pretty much all coaches are up to speed on the importance of the kicking game now. Back when I played, there were still a few teams that didn't put as much work into it. And you could tell which ones they were. You could sense that there was nothing elaborate in their coverage schemes or their blocking schemes, or see that they just didn't put in the effort when you'd watch them on film. But then you'd run into a team like the Bills with Steve Tasker, who was a threat to block a kick every time. He was someone you'd have to keep track of—always. Or a team with a return man like Mel Gray or David

History Book

You'll sometimes hear George Allen called the "Father of Special Teams." While that might be a bit of an exaggeration, there's no doubt that the Pro Football Hall of Fame coach was one of the earliest and most vocal proponents of the importance of the kicking game. When Allen coached the NFL's Los Angeles Rams (1966 to 1970) and Washington Redskins (1971 to 1977), he emphasized special teams more than most coaches. In fact, in 1969 Allen was one of the first two NFL head coaches to hire a full-time assistant coach in charge of special teams (that same year, the Philadelphia Eagles also hired a special-teams coach). The man Allen tabbed to be in charge of his kicking game was Dick Vermeil, who is now the head coach in Kansas City. It's no coincidence that the Chiefs have had some of the strongest special-teams units in the league the past several seasons.

Meggett or Brian Mitchell, players who could break a long runback at any time. Those types of individuals are responsible for the increased amount of coaching, preparation, and game planning that is now necessary to successfully play special teams.

Adam Vinatieri has been clutch for the New England Patriots. His performance during the Pats' Super Bowl run is a big reason New England has won three championships in the last four years.

CHAPTER NINETEEN

The Kickoff

Getting Started

There is more to a kickoff than simply kicking the ball as hard as you can. Some of the kickers will kick directionally; they try to kick it in between the yard numbers and the sidelines so their team can squeeze the coverage. Instead of keeping coverage balanced, with five players covering on one side and five on the other side all going down the field, you have one acting as a runner and swing him over from one of the sides. Now you have six members of the coverage team on the side of the field you're kicking to, and four on the other. The big assumption here, of course, is that your kicker can do a good job and pin the return man on one side of the field.

Other times, maybe when they're going up against a great return man, you see kickers do a sort of bloop kick—high and short. One thing that does is mess with everybody's timing.

Rules to Know

In the NFL the kickoff is made from the kicking team's 30 yard line. In college football teams kick off from their own 35 yard line.

If a kick goes out of bounds before it's touched by anyone on the receiving team (and before it reaches the end zone), the ball belongs to the receiving team 30 yards from the spot of the kick. So, on a normal kickoff in the NFL, the offense would take over at its 40 yard line. In college ball the offense would get it at the 35.

Kickers always tip their hand when they are doing something different. You just can't kick the ball to the right with the exact same approach that you would when you kick the ball to the left. So, when I played in the center spot—the blocker who is positioned directly opposite, and closest to, the kicker—on kickoff returns, Cowboys special-teams coach Joe Avezzano always had me watch the approach of the kickers. Just little things. Maybe the kicker would be a yard farther out from the hash mark if he was going to kick left than he would be if he was kicking right.

At that point I could dictate where our return would go by signaling behind my back. Let's say we've had a right-side return called. If I see they're going to kick it to their right—our left—we need to make sure that we change to a left-side return. If they're going to kick it to the left, we need to keep our return to the right. And I need to make sure that everybody gets that signal, that there's no miscommunication.

One time there was a kicker for the Eagles who was only a yard different in his approach. If he stood on the hash mark, then I knew he was going to kick it to our right. If he stood a yard off the hash, then I knew he was going to kick it to our left. So he picked a spot, and I signaled to our return team. Then he moved, and I signaled again. And then he just kept on going back and forth until we both just stood there and laughed. He knew what he was doing. He was just messing with me.

Covering Kicks

Most important for covering kicks is lane integrity: staying in your lane all the way downfield. Once the ball is kicked and guys are running, you don't want someone on the coverage team to fall in behind another one of your players. The field is 160 feet—53⅓ yards—wide. So every player has about 5 yards that is considered his lane. That's not a real big space. But once you get out of that, you start to have problems: If one guy is running behind another, now it's a 10-yard space. Or maybe there was a double team coming into that area when you got out of your lane, and now you've created a really big hole. So the key on coverage is to never run behind your own teammate or lose your

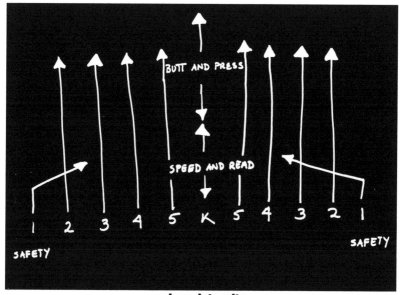

Lane Integrity

lane integrity—because the ball will find its way to the vacated lane.

Mostly, covering kicks is just a question of discipline and effort. You need to know your lane and know exactly where you are. There's an area on the field that Joe Avezzano called the "speed-and-read" zone, where you could get out of your lane because there was still time to get back in it. Kickoffs now are from the 30 yard line, so the speed-and-read zone would extend from there to maybe the opponent's 40 or 45 yard line. In that zone, if your opponent tried to block you, you could go around him and still have time to get back to your lane assignment. But once you got down to the 30 or the 35 yard line, then it was the "butt-and-press" zone. Now you had to take on the blocker, hit him, and get him off you. Just like a linebacker, you had to defeat the block and get after the ballcarrier—in this case the return man. But if you tried to run around a block at that point of the field, like you would in the speed-and-read zone, then you'd be giving up your lane integrity because you'd be too far down the field.

Onside Kicks

Onside kicks are short kickoffs that the kicking team attempts to cover. It needs to travel only 10 yards (unless touched by a player on the receiving team before 10 yards). In an onside kick you usually have two players who are the "catch" guys—usually a wide receiver with good jumping ability or a tight end, players with good hands. These designated catchers are lined up behind the rest of the kickoff team, who are trying to block to give the catchers time to recover the ball without getting hit.

If I'm one of the players who are supposed to block, and I can get a nice Sunday hop, which is gentle and easy to field, and then get down on the ground, I do it. Otherwise I'm assigned to turn and block and let the ball go through to the designated catch guys behind me.

Usually, the kicking team will line up eight players on the kick side and two to the back side. If the receiving team doesn't match the two players on the back side, then there's an opportunity to kick it to the back side and take advantage of that two-on-one situation. If there's nobody back on the second tier, the kicking team can bloop the ball over into the uncovered area and let its two catchers chase it down.

But usually, the receiving team will match the eight guys on the kicking team, and the kicker will hit hard on top of the ball and pop it real high into the air. The receiving team's players on the front side have to block and give their catch guys time to get to the ball. And the setup's the same for the kicking team. It will have players assigned to blow up people and free up others to go get the ball.

I was on the "hands" team in Dallas—the unit that goes out there when you know an onside kick is coming and you need to be sure to cover it. That's the worst of the special teams because sometimes you have eight, nine, ten players bearing down on you when you're trying to field a ball that can take some crazy bounces.

Of course, the best onside kicks are the surprise ones. If you see something in your film study that you can exploit, you could attempt a surprise onside kick early in a game. You know, you might ask, "Do they have anybody who leaves early to get downfield and block? Well, yeah, they do—the tackle over there bails out pretty quick, so we've got a real good shot at it."

In Dallas we had Eddie Murray kick for us a couple of seasons. He was amazing. Before trying an onside kick, he did nothing that would indicate to the opponent what we were planning to do. It would look just like a normal kick to the end zone was coming. Then, at the last second, he'd make an adjustment and do the onside kick.

Sometimes you'll see a kicker kick the ball straight ahead 10 yards. A team will try this type of surprise onside kick when the center on the return team bails out too soon and heads downfield to block. I actually had one of those pulled against me when I was playing center. It's the first thing you guard against, though. You want the other team to see on film that you aren't going to leave too soon. And I wasn't one who ever left too soon. So I don't know why, but the Jets tried it in a game against Dallas one year. It's a hard position to be in because you can't wait for the ball to come to you or travel the 10 yards. If you're the guy who is playing center, you've got to go get it. And you've got four players coming right for you. So even if you do cover the ball, you know you're going to get blown up. I had just that one in my career. It wasn't a lot of fun.

The late Reggie Roby, who played from 1983 to 1999, is considered one of the best punters ever to play in the NFL. He had a very distinct high drop and full follow-through with his kick leg.

Photo courtesy of the Miami Dolphins

CHAPTER TWENTY

Punts

Just Like Golf?

Everybody wants a guy who can punt the ball a country mile with great hang time. But like a kickoff, sometimes it isn't just about punting the ball as far as you can. When punting from near midfield, you don't want the ball to go into the end zone for a touchback, giving your opponents the ball at their 20 yard line. There is an art to placing the ball where you want it. When I played, more guys used to go for the "coffin corner" (because the ball was "buried" deep in the corner). Nowadays, there are only a few guys who will try that. And it's mostly the old guard—punters like Sean Landeta, who's been around forever and is great at it. Today's punters use variations of "sky kicks" where the ball is kicked high into the air and the onus is on the cover guys to down the ball before it goes into the end zone.

On a punt, the coffin corner is the corner created by the out of bounds line on either side of the field closest to the receiving team's end zone. A punter that can directionally punt the ball to this area before it reaches the goal line puts the receiving team in a big hole to start its possession.

Now punters try to drop a kick down near the goal line and have it die there or have a teammate cover it. They have landmarks. The 8 yard line is one. If you're kicking it from around midfield, or on the opponent's side of the field, the return man is going to stand at the 8 yard line. That's his spot. He's never supposed to go backward. If it goes over his head, he's instructed to let it go. So, if you've got a punter who can drop it between the 8 yard line and goal line, you're going to get a lot of balls that get downed in there. But that's still pretty difficult. I've heard a lot of these punters say it's just like playing golf. Think of it just like sticking a wedge in there down near the goal line, they tell me. But I don't buy that. It's just not that easy. You've got to teach me to get my wedge within 8 yards of the hole every time!

Fake Punts

A fake punt works best when you're in your end of the field, down around your 30 yard line or so. You want the other team to be in a block situation if you're running a fake. You'll hear players say a fake works best from around midfield, but I don't think they work well there, because often the opposing team is on the alert for a fake, and its regular defense could be on the field. So the best time to try a fake is when you're in your own end. But if you want to run a fake punt, you'd better have a good defense in which you've got a lot of confidence. Because if the fake doesn't work, then you're giving your opponent a short field to work with.

I ran the ball on a fake punt one time up at Washington in 1992. I was the up back and took a direct snap and went 13 yards for a first down. It turned out to be one of the longest runs of my career. I had a lot of fun with that.

Punt Protection

Protecting on punts is harder than protecting on field goals or extra

Moose's Memories

Usually I played the wing, on the outside, on punts for the Cowboys. Bill Bates, a safety, was normally the personal protector (the blocking back who is positioned between the line of scrimmage and the punter). But one year Bill tore a ligament in his knee early in the season, so they had me take over as the personal protector. And that turned out to be the year we went to the Super Bowl for the first time (the 1992 season) in my career. And we actually had the first punt of Super Bowl XXVII against Buffalo blocked.

You could see it coming, too. After we went three and out the first time we had the ball, Mike Saxon came in to punt. But the Bills overloaded one side with Steve Tasker to the back side. Their formation isolated him in that situation, giving him a lot of room to work with because of the way we would block their punt rush. And he's so fast that he got in there and blocked the ball out of bounds at our 16 yard line. Buffalo scored four plays later to take the lead, but we still ended up winning the game, 52–17.

points because much more time elapses between the snap of the ball and the kick. So, on punts you've got to be able to engage your blocks; you've got to be able to stay with your man. And sometimes that's tough, especially if you're blocking someone who is quick on the outside. Take Steve Tasker. He was a perennial Pro Bowl player on special teams for the Buffalo Bills. He was so quick. He could freeze you and go around you, then still have enough time to get back inside and block a kick.

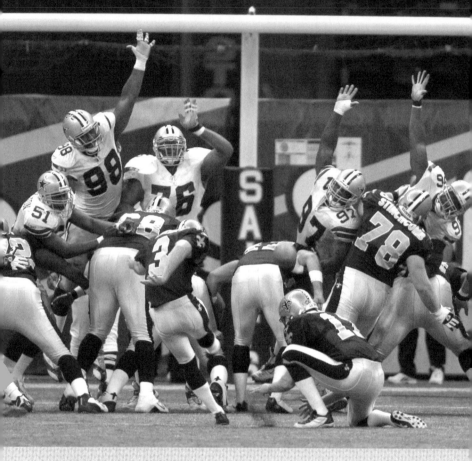

A reliable kicker is more important than ever in today's NFL. Parity has made games closer than ever, and a good kicker can be the difference in a team's season.

Photo courtesy of the *Dallas Cowboys Official Weekly*

CHAPTER TWENTY-ONE

Field Goals and Extra Points

Mind Games

How many times do we see it? Two teams fight tooth and nail for more than fifty-nine minutes, and then a kicker comes on at the end and makes a field goal to win the game—or misses a field goal and his team loses the game.

The most important thing about a kicker is his mental makeup. He must be able to handle the knowledge that his team is counting on him to win a game—and it could be a critical game. It's like having someone in basketball who wants the ball in his hands at the end of the game to take that three-pointer. You want a kicker who relishes the opportunity to go out on the field and kick the winning field goal at the end of the game. He's not nervous about the situation, and he doesn't care about the conditions. Once the kick is called for, he just thinks, "Great! I get to go out there and win this game and be the hero."

Look at Adam Vinatieri: He won two Super Bowls for the Patriots with field goals in the closing seconds, and he won a lot of games for them on the way to those Super Bowls, too. On the other hand, look at Scott Norwood. He missed a field goal at the end of Super Bowl XXV, and Buffalo lost to the New York Giants by a single point. His kick was 47 yards, so it was no gimme. But you wonder: If he made that field goal, what happens to the Bills? Do they still go on to lose the next three Super Bowls, too, or do they win a couple of those games?

If a kicker misses a kick at the end and his team loses the game, everyone is always going to look at that play. But here's my feeling: There were probably five or six plays during the course of a game

Rules to Know

The goalposts in the NFL are 18 feet, 6 inches wide, and the crossbar is 10 feet above the ground. The posts are directly in line with the hash marks on the field.

The width of the goalposts is the same in college now as it is in the pros, but the position of the hash marks is still different. They're closer to the sidelines in college football, meaning a field-goal try in college can be from a much different angle than you'll ever find in the NFL.

that—had they turned out differently—should have prevented that team from getting to the point where the kicker had to try the field goal to win it. And even if he makes the kick and his team does win, it's the same thing. There are so many other plays that go into it, and if your team is making those plays, the game should not be that close.

When Good Kickers Go Bad

It's like the yips to a golfer. A kicker misses a couple, and it gets into his head. He just loses that confidence. Tampa Bay's Martin Gramatica was one of the best kickers in the game a few years ago. He made thirty-two field goals in 2002 when the Buccaneers won the Super Bowl. All of a sudden, he started missing almost as many field goals as he made, and he lost his job in the 2004 season.

Then you look at kickers like Jason Elam, who's been in Denver since 1993 and is unbelievably consistent. Jason Hanson has been in Detroit for years. And Vinatieri—not only did he make the winning field goals for New England in the Super Bowls, but he also kicked one in the snow to beat the Raiders in the 2001 playoffs. Under those conditions with the wind and the snow, and because a missed kick would have ended the Patriots' season, he says that was the best kick he's ever made. There was a kick he made against Tennessee in the playoffs in 2003 that also was just ridiculous.

The K-Ball

A few years ago, the NFL began requiring kickers to use a "K-ball." These are new footballs sealed in a special box and not opened until they're delivered to the officials' locker room shortly before game time.

It used to be that the footballs were given to the teams on the Wednesday before the game. They had until Sunday to get the balls in the shape they wanted. It was amazing the things they could do to them—hit 'em around a racquetball court or with a baseball bat, put them in a dryer, throw 'em against the wall—to soften them up. They'd get the footballs brand new, and by game time the balls looked like they were five years old. They were good to go.

When kickers were kicking off from the 35 yard line and they were doctoring the balls, everything went into the end zone. Now, with the K-balls fresh out of the box and the kickoffs from the 30, fewer kicks go into the end zone. Still, you've got to hand it to the kickers. Even with the K-ball, you still see a lot of long field goals these days.

The Holder and Snapper

It's important for the kicker to get accustomed to his holder and the snapper. But that's really not a big deal. It's going to be the same everywhere. If a kicker pulls a quad muscle on Saturday, you should be able to go out and find someone to come in and kick for you on Sunday. It just shouldn't be an issue. There are only thirty-two kicking jobs, so there are always some good kickers out there.

In Dallas we changed kickers a lot. We had Ken Willis, then Lin Elliott, Eddie Murray, Chris Boniol, Richie Cunningham. We went through a different kicker every two, three years. The organization's approach was, we can always find somebody who is going to work out. In one stretch we had a lot of young kickers. It's a position where you can often go with a young player, and you can save some salary-cap money.

Punters are starting to take over the position of holder from the backup quarterback. It's just because there's not enough time—not enough time for him to build a chemistry with the kicker. When the quarterbacks are out there running the game plan, the kicker is working somewhere else with the snapper and the holder. The best situation is to have your punter be the holder because kickers have all the down time together. Sometimes the punter becomes your holder just because while all the other players are working on different things in practice, he's got time to work on the snap and the kick. So he just kind of works his way into the job.

Blocking Kicks

Sometimes kicks are blocked, figuratively speaking, in the film room. What do teams see then that makes them feel they can block a kick? Effort—or, rather, lack of it. They might see a player who is lazy and takes a play off or somebody who uses poor technique. I can still hear Joe Avezzano, our special-teams coach in Dallas, talking in the film room: "We've got a shot on the wing here because their end is lazy." Or, "We can pressure that gap," because the guard's technique isn't sound.

Most of the blocks that I can remember during my career came from the outside, off the wing. But you see a lot of blocked kicks in the game today that come from the interior of the line. One technique is to kind of pull your opponent as you go forward to prevent him from getting to his assignment. A player using bad technique is susceptible to being grabbed and prevented from being able to block his assignment. Sometimes the long snapper is an undersize guy, and you can put a bigger lineman over him and make it a mismatch.

But again, for the most part it gets back to film study. What do you see on film? Can you beat your opponent with a quick move in the gap? Do the linemen lock behind? That is, sometimes the players on the offensive line lock their feet, and if you can get a really good push, they'll fall back on top of each other. Get a big push and let your designated leaper get a few yards closer to jump and block the kick. On

A blocked kick can alter the complexion of a game. One special-teams miscue can offset a good offensive and defensive performance.

Photo courtesy of the
Dallas Cowboys Official Weekly

the outside teams will try to force the wing into a situation where he has to block two kick rushers. The rush team will grab the end and pull him down to the inside creating a bigger area for the wing to protect and eliminating any help from the end on the inside rusher. That way, you'd create a situation in which you've forced the wing man to block two guys. One of them could get through and block the kick.

There are different ways to attack. But everything goes back to the starting point, and that's what you see on film and know you can exploit.

Kick Protection

The cardinal rule, whether on punts or placekicks, is don't get beat inside. That's the number one thing. Don't let your opponent cross your face and get to your inside. On a field goal or extra point, avoiding that doesn't take a whole lot. Just get a good stiff arm on your opponent, and he's not going to be able to get there in time. If the mechanics are good from snapper to holder to kicker, it's only about 1.6 seconds, 1.8 seconds to get the kick off. It's a pretty tough chore for the defense to beat that. Up front, you don't want to surge forward, and you don't want your weight back on your heels. You've got to keep your balance and also keep your shoulders square. You don't want your shoulders turned due to poor technique or because you were grabbed by a defender.

History Book

The longest field goal in NFL history is 63 yards. Jason Elam made a kick that far to end the first half for Denver in a victory over Jacksonville in 1998. That tied the mark set twenty-eight years earlier by New Orleans' Tom Dempsey in a game against Detroit. The remarkable thing about Dempsey is that he was born with only half a right foot (and no right hand). He wore a specially made shoe. Dempsey's long field goal not only was record shattering, but it was dramatic, too. It came as time ran out, and it gave the Saints a 19–17 win.

Fake Field Goals

The way I see it, if you're going to fake a field goal, then you might as well just go ahead and line up and go for it on fourth down. Fake field goals don't work all that well unless you really see something that jumps out at you on film. Unless you're up against a team that's not doing something they should be doing from an assignment standpoint, then a fake field goal is a waste of time. On the defensive side, if everybody does his job, a fake field goal should never work.

Brian Mitchell is second in the NFL to Jerry Rice in all-time combined yards (rushing, receiving, kick returns), ahead of players like Jim Brown and Emmitt Smith. The majority of Mitchell's yards came on punt and kick returns.

Photo courtesy of The Washington Redskins

Returns

Kickoff Returns

You're starting to see more and more teams making big plays in the return game. But what it all comes down to in the return game is effort. Look at a club like Philadelphia: You look back at special-teams rankings the past three or four years, and the Eagles are consistently there. For a long time in Philly, there was a little emphasis on special teams. But since John Harbaugh got there as the special-teams coach in 1998, there's been a lot more attention paid to them. The same is true with Atlanta. It's amazing what good special-teams play can do for a team that is struggling. Or maybe a team that is favored to win, but comes out a little flat—a big return can get them back on track.

Basically, on kickoff returns you're just trying to punch a hole in the coverage. It's mainly about double teams—utilizing a double team to try to create a lane on the return. It's just the opposite of covering kicks. You want to stay in your 5-yard lane in coverage; you want to get your opponent out of that lane on the return.

On our returns in Dallas, we always planned for two double teams. If we saw that a certain player on the outside was loafing, he didn't run hard out there on the coverage, then we could forget about him. We'd figure we're not even going to put a blocker on him, and that way we could go somewhere else to get three double teams. If there's a weak link, it's going to pop up on film in a hurry.

On most returns you're going to set up a wedge in front of the return man. The players in the back are going to form the wedge, and the coverage team will have unblocked men running free to the wedge. On middle returns it is usually the two players closest to the kicker. On side returns it is usually the two outside guys to the side of the return.

When the wedge and the wedge buster meet, the result is one of the most violent collisions on the field every Sunday. What people don't understand about kickoff returns is that you're retreating about 35 yards. And then you turn around, and you've got to try to stop someone who's running a 45-yard sprint, just stop him in his tracks. And those players in the back on the return team, a lot of them are reserve offensive linemen, and they're not accustomed to blocking a man in space, in the open field. To be on the move and block another guy who's on the move like that—well, it's a totally different form of blocking for them. So a lot of times, you see that wedge buster come down and make an offensive lineman miss. Sometimes they just try to blow up the lineman. And those guys get dinged up so bad they might have to sit out a couple of series. Like I said, it takes a certain mentality to play special teams.

Daryl's Best

Kansas City's Dante Hall and Detroit's Eddie Drummond are probably the two best return men in the league today. Hall returned 4 kicks—2 punts and 2 kickoffs—for touchdowns in 2003. Drummond brought back 3 consecutive kicks—2 punts and a kickoff—all the way in 2004. That was something that had never been done before. I like J. R. Reed from the Eagles, too. He has a great mentality for the return game: no fear. He has faith that the players in front of him are going to get the blocking done, and he hits the hole at 100 miles per hour. R. W. McQuarters and Jerry Azumah gave Chicago a great one-two punch on punts and kickoffs—this played very well to the Bears' style, which relied on special teams and defense.

Dante Hall didn't have quite the year in 2004 that he had in 2003, but maybe the blockers up front didn't have quite the same year, either. It's like everything else in football: Chemistry and confidence play a big part in the return game. The kick returner has to believe that his teammates up front are going to make the blocks for him.

Blocking for a Kickoff Return

The center position on the kickoff-return unit is the hardest because you're not going straight back and you are usually not part of a double team. Depending on whether you've got a right return or a left return on, you're going back at an angle to that side. So you've got to have a landmark to go to when you're leaving. There's a lot more to it than turning around and running. You've got your back to the guys who are going downfield to try to make the tackle. Did they cross? Let's say in prekick I was on number 58. Now I've turned around to run and he's crossed with his teammate, so who do I have now?

When you block, you count players. Your blocking assignments go from the wide side in—right 1, 2, 3, 4, 5; left 1, 2, 3, 4, 5. As the center, I had R5 or L5 predominately. I'd start to run back and then I'd turn around, and all of a sudden, the players have switched. The guy who was number 5 became number 4, and the one who was number 4 has crossed behind him to become number 5. The key to deciphering this is film study. You see on film that they come running down after the kick about 7 yards, then they switch. It doesn't really do anything to mess you up as long as you're prepared for it because you don't block the man, you block the assignment. I would adjust and block the player who became number 5.

You might think that a successful blocker on the kick-return team will just try to go for the kill shot, really flatten his opponent, but there's a lot more that goes into it. You want to get back into position to get the best leverage that you can. If we're taking our return to the near sideline, you're going to take on your man, keeping your butt between the returner and your assignment. At some point the cover man will stop and retrace to try to get to the returner. As a blocker you must maintain your balance and keep your leverage.

Punt Returns

It's not just pure speed that makes a great punt returner. It's the ability to avoid a tackle and the ability to go north and south. The key is evading the initial tackler. You don't need to have someone who is

Gridiron Glossary

Going **north and south** isn't a strict directional term, of course; it just means taking it to the defense and moving from goal line to goal line instead of sideline to sideline. (In the old days most stadiums were built so the field ran north-south, but especially with the advent of indoor stadiums, that's not necessarily true anymore.)

fast enough to steer clear of four or five tacklers during the course of a return, just someone you're sure can avoid that first tackler bearing down on him.

Brian Mitchell, who played fourteen years in the NFL with three different teams, was one of the greatest return men ever to play the game, and he didn't have blazing speed. His great talent was the ability to break tackles. He was very difficult to get down on the ground.

Players like Mel Gray and Eric Metcalf, they were a different breed. They were speedsters, but they could avoid tackles, too. Deion Sanders did it with a change of pace and a burst. With his speed he could get up into the field, then actually break to the outside, lose ground again, and still have the confidence that he was going to turn the corner. Dave Meggett had speed and strength, and he was really good at setting up blockers. He was one of those kick returners who was real good at making the initial defender miss, too.

Blocking for a Punt Return

Sometimes it's not fair for the punt returners, because if you're going to try to block a punt, you're not going to be able to set up a return. So, if the return man can do anything in that situation, you've got a real special player. More often that not, though, if the emphasis is on blocking a kick, the return man is going to be instructed to call for a fair catch, especially if there is any kind of hang time on the kick. There is just no way that the fielding team can get upfield to pressure the punter, then back downfield to block for the returner.

Moose's Memories

Without a doubt the one player we always had to be wary of in Dallas when covering kicks was Mel Gray. He played for several NFL teams in a twelve-year career that ended in 1997. One year, Mike Saxon, our punter, got the game ball because we gave up no yardage on punt returns to Gray. Mike kicked away from Gray the whole game, and his punts landed right on the sideline. Mike did a great job. He was excellent at directional kicking.

When you have a return set up, you have to be able to take advantage of the situation by establishing a running lane. But it's up to the return man to make one defender—the first one, the guy who's trying to knock him off his feet—miss. If he can do that, and his blockers are busting their tails, then there's a pretty decent chance that something good can come out of the return.

Most of the big returns nowadays go straight up the middle. Or maybe up the middle for 10 or 15 yards, then they break to the sideline. You don't see a whole lot of the old-fashioned returns, when a team would set up a wall on the outside and the return man would turn the corner and head on down the sideline untouched.

Rules to Know

Here's a little-known rule that occasionally will come into play. The receiving team is entitled to a free kick after any fair catch. Obviously, that's rare. After almost every fair catch, the offense will opt for a regular play from scrimmage. But you can see that it might be beneficial to take advantage of the rule. Say a team punts from near its own end zone late in the closing seconds of a half or the game. The receiving team could call for a fair catch, then try a field goal unimpeded. San Francisco coach Bill Walsh exercised the option one year at the end of the first half of a 1988 divisional playoff game against Minnesota. Punt returner John Taylor made a fair catch at midfield, and kicker Mike Cofer came on to try a 60-yard field goal with no center snap and no pass rush. The kick fell short.

During the season, home for professional football players is a 4-foot-wide cubby.

Photo by Ron St. Angelo

E.SMITH
22

RRIS

· 8 TROY AIKMAN

A Player's Life

I have three Super Bowl Championships and two Pro Bowl appearances, but I am most proud of my family. Evan sits on Diane, and I'm holding Aidan.

Mooooose

The Name

Everyone wants to know how I got the nickname "Moose." It was Babe Laufenberg, a backup quarterback in Dallas for a couple of seasons, who gave it to me in my rookie year of 1989.

In Dallas the coaches would give the offensive players the game plan as a group, then we would split up into positions—quarterbacks, running backs, receivers, and tight ends. In our individual meetings we would go over the game plan more in depth, then come back together and meet as a group again.

Our group, the running backs, was always the last to come back in. And pretty much all of the running backs for the Cowboys at the time were under 6' tall and weighed 180, 185 pounds (Emmitt Smith, who was just 5'9" but weighed 207 pounds, wasn't there yet). And then there was me at 6'2" and 238 pounds. When we came walking back en masse into the offensive meeting together, I guess I kind of stood out from the others. Babe saw me one day and said, "You look like a moose walking in a field of deer when you come back in."

And the rest, as they say, is history.

A Sense of Belonging?

I grew up in Youngstown, New York, but I followed the Miami Dolphins. Larry Csonka—the Dolphins burly, rumbling fullback—was my man. He was a powerful running back who wasn't afraid to bowl over a defender when he had to, but he could utilize his quickness, too. (Csonka, Jim Kiick, Paul Warfield—those were some great Miami teams of the 1970s. But when those guys all went to the World Football League, I didn't even watch. That league didn't even exist as far as I was concerned.)

I never expected I'd be playing on some of the same fields in the same NFL stadiums those guys did. And once I got to college, and then even into the pros, I always had it in the back of my mind, "Do I really belong here?"

I know for a fact, because I've had this confirmed, that coming out of Lewiston-Porter High School in Youngstown in 1984, I was offered the last scholarship at Syracuse. I was not highly recruited out of high school—really, no big school came after me—and I only got the scholarship to Syracuse because someone who had originally committed there backed out and went to another school. Then in Dallas, even though I was a second-round draft pick, that doubt still was always there, and it was something that really motivated me.

In my first two years in Dallas, I wasn't really comfortable with the system we had. Then the Cowboys brought in offensive coordinator Norv Turner, and the other guys and I—I've talked to tight end Jay Novacek about this—all felt that our abilities at our positions were a perfect match for Norv's system.

That first season in Dallas was tough for a lot of other reasons, too. For one thing football is really big in Texas, and that took some getting used to. Then there was the whole Tom Landry thing going on—Landry had been the only coach in Cowboys history until Jerry Jones bought the club and hired Jimmy Johnson in 1989. We were kind of caught in the middle of all that with people taking sides, and we won only one game all season.

It sure didn't feel like we were heading in the right direction. A lot of people forget that in the second year (Jimmy Johnson's second year as coach and my second year as a player), we won only 3 of our first 10 games. So after 26 games we were 4–22. But then we got it going after that. We rallied to finish 7–9, and two years later we were playing in the Super Bowl.

Rules to Know

A player is not eligible for the NFL until three years after his high school class has graduated. Running back Maurice Clarett challenged that rule before the 2004 draft but lost in the courts. That's been different from the NBA, where players could be drafted right out of high school. But starting with the 2006 draft, players must be nineteen to join a pro basketball team. While there are a lot of reasons for this type of deferment, physically, you need a lot more time to prepare for the NFL. I was prepared coming out of college. I had redshirted—practiced with the team but didn't play in a game, so I retained the year of eligibility—as a freshman, so I was at Syracuse for five years. By the time I was drafted, I was ready physically for the NFL. You see a lot of players leaving college after their junior years now, and they're not physically ready, nor do they have the fundamental skills that players entering the NFL used to have.

Daryl's dad, Peter aka Butch (holding M), and mom, Ann (OO), along with friends Gil Tomei (S) and Don Schlosser (E), root for the team.

Photo courtesy of Ann Johnston

Dealing with the Fans

The off-field stuff—autograph seekers, dealing with fans, the media attention—goes with the job description. It's part of the privilege and the responsibility of being a professional football player or, in my case now, a broadcaster.

Autograph Seekers

Now I'm not going to lie and say I'm always accommodating to people asking for autographs. There have been times when I've been short. Sometimes I think people just have to realize that you could be in the middle of a bad day. There's also a time and a place for everything. If I'm having dinner with my wife and my children, and a fan comes up to me and asks for an autograph just as the food is brought to our table, then I'm probably not going to be very welcoming.

I try to make myself as available as possible and as accommodating as I can be, but I know there have been times when I haven't. Take training camp, for instance. Our training camps in Texas (in Austin and Wichita Falls) were a fiasco. It was great that the fans would get involved and get to see us up close and all, but when I'm coming off the field after spending two and a half hours in 103 degree heat, well, the last thing I want to do is go over and sign a whole bunch of autographs.

And, as a player, if you do walk away, you feel bad. But Bernie Kosar, who played quarterback in Dallas in 1993, taught me something early in my NFL career. He said instead of trying to justify your position on why you don't want to do something, just do it. By the time you get through all that about why you can't or won't do it, you could have just signed the cap or the T-shirt or the piece of paper, and the fans would have been gone, thinking you were a great guy.

Kids Come First

I always tried to accommodate little kids. I've never—I hope I can say this in all honesty—turned down a child's request for an autograph. You would hope the adults would understand, but nine times out of ten, it's kids who are the polite ones. They are very appreciative, and they are very patient when they're in a group.

It's the adults who push their way up front and pass things over the heads of the children. I love to get in those situations, though, because as I'm signing, I'm always observing. And a lot of times, I'll walk away and someone will say, "But you didn't sign mine!" And I'll say, "Well, do you realize you pushed two kids out of the way and then you shoved the cap in my face when I asked you to let them go first?" I do have certain rules for those situations.

If a 4-foot cubby is a player's home during the season, this is his home in the off-season. Football has become a year-round sport with strength and conditioning programs starting in March and ending just before training camp. This is only the entrance to the Dallas weight room.

Photo courtesy of the *Dallas Cowboys Official Weekly*

A Player's Calendar

A Player's Week

Every team is a little bit different, of course, but the way we ran things in Dallas when I was playing there was representative of a typical week for an NFL player. Here's how the week would go.

Monday

The day after a game, we'd get in early, work out, doing a little light weight lifting. Early afternoon, we'd have a team meeting, watch some game tapes, then get onto the field for some light conditioning. We were done early.

Tuesday

Tuesday is the players' day off. But I would go in to do my lower-body workouts. On Monday I was too sore from the game to do it. By Tuesday I was beginning to feel a little better, and I didn't want to put them off until Wednesday or Thursday because those were our heavy days of practice. Then it was sit in the cold tub, sit in the hot tub, and try to hang out and get over the punishment you took on Sunday.

Wednesday

Wednesday was the longest day, the heaviest day. I'd get in a little before 8:00 A.M., maybe 7:50 or so, and sit in the hot tub, still trying to work out the kinks. Special teams would meet at 8:45, then the offense's meeting started at 9:30. That went until about 10:45. Then it was onto the field for a walk-through with the offense and the special teams at 11:00 before time for some lunch and a workout. From 1:00

to 1:30 P.M. we'd watch film, which I always hated—not watching the film, but the timing of it. You'd be sitting in a dark room having just eaten lunch. All you wanted to do was fall asleep. Plus, it was right before we'd head out to the practice field, so it made for a pretty sluggish start at practice. We were on the field from 1:45 until about 4:00 or 4:15. Then we had half an hour from the time we left the practice field to be in the meeting rooms again and go over the practice tapes. We'd finish up the day around 5:30 or so.

Thursday

Thursday was pretty much the same schedule as Wednesday, but with some different emphasis on the practice field. The third-down passing game was installed, and you worked on the two-minute drill to finish practice.

Friday

We'd report at the same time on Friday morning, but it was a lighter day, and a faster one. Special teams still met from 8:45 to 9:30, and offense after that. But Friday was kind of our specialty practice—short-yardage, goal-line, red-zone situations. It was a polished practice, and we were on the field from about 11:00 to 12:30. Then it was in to watch the practice tape again, but on Fridays you were out of there by about 1:45. It was pretty much a half day.

Moose's Memories

Sometimes things would happen on the practice field and you'd think, "Oh, brother, now I've got to go see this on tape." But at least that was just with your position guys. It was a lot worse with games. On Monday the team watched the game tape as a group, and sometimes you'd think, "Ugh. I don't want to see that again." Of course, on the flip side, sometimes you'd made a really good play and then you couldn't wait for your teammates to see it on tape.

Saturday

Saturday was a travel day if we were playing on the road. If we were at home, we got in around 10:00 A.M. for some meetings, then a walk-through on the field. All fine-tuning stuff, nothing heavy.

Sunday

Game day. Playing on Monday night threw everything a little off kilter for the rest of the week. If we happened to be playing on a Monday, then we would just add an extra Wednesday into the week. So Wednesday would be Wednesday, but Thursday would be Wednesday, too. Everything would back up one day after that. So basically, we were adding an extra day of heavy practice. It was bad enough to have two!

Training Camp

Football is a year-round game for a player these days, from off-season workouts to minicamps and everything else. It used to be that guys would take a job in the off-season, then come back for training camp in July to get back into shape for the season. Of course, the money is so much better now that no one needs to take another job to make ends meet—but training camp is still training camp.

There is nothing good about training camp—no, I take that back. The end of camp is the only thing good about it. That's it. It's two-a-day practices in one hundred degree heat, and there is just nothing good about that.

I was never in better shape the entire year than I was the day I walked into camp. And I was never in worse shape the entire year than the day I walked out of training camp. I have no idea why they do that. It would literally take me until the first week of October even to get close to the shape I was in before camp started.

Guys miss training camp all the time now. In Seattle Walter Jones reports late almost every year. Teams put the franchise tag on guys and the players say, "Fine, see you when camp is over." Jimmy Johnson (he coached the Cowboys from 1989 to 1993) wouldn't let anyone get away with that. He either would have showed up for camp or found himself playing for another team.

Jimmy, in fact, had us in camp one year for twenty-one days straight. He had decided early on in his first year in 1989 that he was going to go back to doing things the way he did them in college. He got a lot more aggressive with his practice schedule, and in 1990 we had that long stretch. We actually went in and told him it was against union rules—you're supposed to have one day in every seven-day period completely free from football, no practices, meetings, nothing. But he said he was going to do it until someone told him he couldn't, and we ended up at twenty-one days before we had a day off. I don't think anybody from the league came to talk to him; I think he realized we needed a break.

Jimmy also was the one who started the whole thing with minicamps. But he called them "quarterback schools." The way he got around the rules was that the quarterback schools had to be voluntary. They couldn't be mandatory. But you got the idea pretty quickly that you had better be there or it wasn't going to go over too well.

Monday Night Football

In the beginning everyone got up for playing on a Monday night. But that was early on. Then it got old. I have to be honest; it's nice to be playing in a featured game in front of everyone in the whole country on Monday night, but there's nothing worse than sitting in a hotel room all day long waiting around for the game.

The other thing that playing on a Monday does is it throws a monkey wrench into your normal routine. When we were in our groove in Dallas, we were on *Monday Night Football* three times a year. And mainly, they were games played on the East Coast, which puts you back into Dallas at 3:30 A.M. Tuesday, then, is just an absolute wash because you have to readjust your clock. Now all your workouts are pushed back. In my case Tuesday was my day to do my lower-body workout—squats—but there was no way I was going to be able to do that. I'd still want to do that workout as soon as I could because I

Chatting with Al Michaels before a **Monday Night** *game. I grew up watching* **Monday Night Football** *but never thought that one day I would be playing on that stage.*

Photo by Ron St. Angelo

didn't want to be tired later in the week. So I'd get up early on Wednesday to go do squats, which is really not good because they leave your legs heavy for practice.

Thanksgiving Day

One of the traditions in the NFL is that the Dallas Cowboys (as well as the Detroit Lions) host a game every year on Thanksgiving Day. The tradition started long before I began playing in Dallas—the Cowboys have had a Turkey Day game every year since 1966.

That Thursday comes along pretty quickly after a Sunday game. But it's just like anything else: You get yourself mentally ready for it. Instead of a light day on Monday and an off day on Tuesday, those days were pretty heavy days. Wednesday was a polish practice, but the coaches still keep you moving.

It was easier for us because we didn't have to travel. I think it was much harder for the visiting team. A short week definitely favors the home team. It's more surprising to see a good home team get beat by a struggling traveling team than it is for a good traveling team to go and handle a team that isn't having such a good year. In 2003 visiting Green Bay got beat by a beleaguered Detroit team, which is maybe not as big a shock as someone coming in and winning, like when Miami beat us in 1993, which was probably the best team we had in Dallas in the 1990s.

Of course, the ten days between the Thanksgiving Day game and the following Sunday game made for a nice break—although when you think about it, we really only had Friday, Saturday, and Sunday off. Then it was back to the field on Monday, and we'd do a little bit more on that day than we normally would on a Monday. Still, it was beneficial when we wanted to make a push in December.

Super Bowl Week

In Dallas our coaches always did a real good job of keeping the same schedule for the team during Super Bowl week. They did the best they possibly could at keeping the game in perspective. And that's hard. You're in another city. And you know where you're at—it's the *Super Bowl.*

The first time I took the field as part of a Super Bowl team was in January 1993 at the Rose Bowl in Pasadena, California. And we were all really nervous. Our opponent, the Buffalo Bills, had a lot of experienced veterans who had been there before—in fact this was their third consecutive Super Bowl—while we had one of the youngest teams in the league that season. And we were kind of tight.

We looked over at the Bills when we were lined up for the national anthem, and they were really relaxed. And then the jets did their flyby. You could see the demeanor on our sideline change. Everyone got really excited. Their guys, it just didn't affect them at all. We've always kidded around about that, but the first time you see one of those flybys, it is awesome.

Despite all the hoopla, though, once the ball is kicked off, it becomes just like any other game. As I said, we were a young team that had never been in the Super Bowl before, and the Bills were making their third consecutive appearance, yet they made all the mistakes and we won going away, 52–17. Thank goodness for the flyby. And our defense.

PART SEVEN

Coaches

As the coach, Jimmy Johnson was the architect of Dallas' Super Bowl teams, and the plans started with franchise quarterback Troy Aikman. Jimmy had a vision of what we could accomplish as a team that even as players we didn't see.

Photo by Ron St. Angelo

At some point in every player's career, a special coach makes an impact. For me it was Jim Hofher, now the head coach at SUNY at Buffalo. Jim made football fun for me again at Syracuse (1987–88).

Photo by Ann Johnston

CHAPTER TWENTY-FIVE

Every Coach Is Different

In My Experience

Every head coach is different. Some NFL coaches get closer to their players than others. In Dallas I never interacted with the head coach a whole lot. I played for Jimmy Johnson (from 1989 to 1993), Barry Switzer (1994 to 1997), and Chan Gailey (1998 to 1999). And they were all different. Jimmy, for instance, had a background in defense, while Chan had a background in the offensive side of the game. I dealt with Chan a lot more than I ever did the other two coaches because he was the offensive coordinator and would be in on a lot more of our meetings. Jimmy, on the other hand, pretty much turned over the whole offense to Norv Turner, so I didn't really see him very much. Same thing with Barry. There wasn't a whole lot of interaction there.

Most of the guys that a player is around are his strength coach, his special-teams coach, his offensive or defensive coordinator, and his position coach.

The Position Coach

Position coaches know that there aren't a whole lot of things that they can teach a player who has already made it to the NFL level. So for the most part, they work with you on fundamentals and make sure you know all your assignments in the game plans.

In Dallas our running backs coach, Joe Brodsky, was great. He was like your dad. There were certain things he'd get on you about, tell you over and over. He was always telling me to block a guy right

I had an opportunity to play for three head coaches while I was a Dallas Cowboy. Unfortunately Tom Landry was not one of them.

between the numbers on his jersey. "Why did you take his shoulder?" he would ask me. "You've got to take this guy straight in the numbers and take him backwards." But you know, when a guy weighs 250 or 255 pounds and he's going from left to right, I'm just not going to be able to get him going backwards every time. So that's when I'd take his shoulder and wheel him right out of the play. I'd use his momentum to take him past the hole and give my running back a bigger hole. Still, there was Joe the next day telling me I had to take him "straight in the numbers"!

Joe would always get on Emmitt Smith about his habit of carrying the ball in his right hand all the time, even when he was running left. "You've got to switch the ball to your outside hand," he'd say. But he never forced us. He never told Emmitt how to run. And he never criticized him if he cut back, it didn't work out, and he lost a yard. He would never say, "You've got to stay in this place," or "You can only cut back here." He was terrific that way. He let you be you, and then he would be there whenever you needed him. He'd always be there to watch film with you, and he could give you some really good tips. And any question that he didn't have an answer to, he'd go and get it for you. He was just a good person to be around.

And aside from just being there for you, there's not a whole lot that a position coach can do, at least as far as instruction. His main goal is to make sure that everyone is on the same page. The game plan comes from the coordinator, who explains it to the position coaches; then the position coaches take it to their guys and make sure there's no confusion.

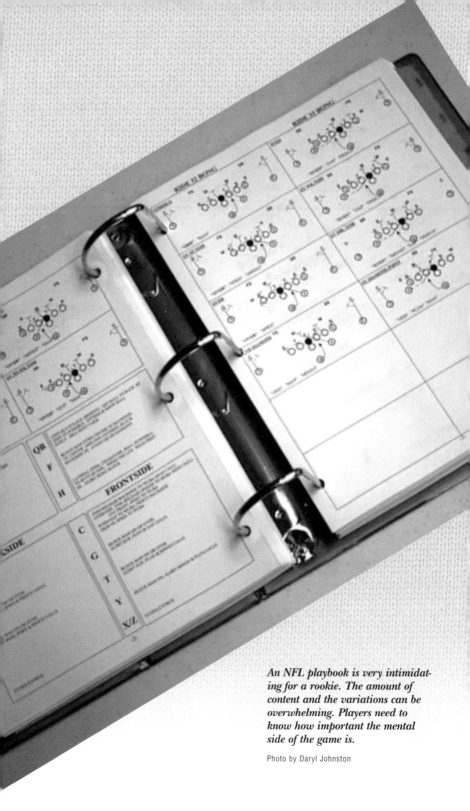

An NFL playbook is very intimidating for a rookie. The amount of content and the variations can be overwhelming. Players need to know how important the mental side of the game is.

Photo by Daryl Johnston

CHAPTER TWENTY-SIX

The Game Plan

Wednesday Morning

Coaches bring in the game plan on Wednesday, and on Wednesday morning you start to work on the different situations that will occur during the game. First and second down, the nickel package (third-down plays), the ball inside the opponent's 20 yard line, blitz drill, inside run, seven on seven—each day a part of the overall plan is emphasized.

The game plan results from a collaboration of all the coaches. As players, we had no input. I don't even know how much input you could say a guy like quarterback Troy Aikman had. The game plan would go in, and Norv Turner or Ernie Zampese (they each had stints as the Cowboys' offensive coordinator in my time in Dallas) would sit with Troy and say, "Okay, on a third-and-plus-7 situation, here are the plays we're going to run. On third and short here is what we've got in mind." They might ask him which ones he likes and which ones he's not too keen on. And they'd take notes on that and keep it in mind when the situation came up in the game. They'd certainly want some sort of feedback so at least they'd know not to call plays that they knew Troy really didn't feel comfortable with in a given situation.

Stick with It

One thing I really liked about Cowboys' offensive coordinators Ernie Zampese and Norv Turner was that on Saturday night they knew what we were going to do on Sunday, and then we went out and did it. And they were very open with us about how the game was going to go.

If we planned to throw the ball early on, they would come right out and tell the offensive line and the running back, "You are going to have to be patient because we are going to come out and establish the pass first. It doesn't make sense for us to run ourselves into a brick wall in the first quarter, so we're going to try to loosen these guys up. We're not going to abandon the run, though—in fact we're going to wear them down when we use it in the second half." And then there were games when they told us they were going to put the onus on the running game. "We know that they are really good with what they do from a cover standpoint, and they pressure the quarterback and have a good blitz package, so we don't want to be dropping back and throwing the ball. You guys have got to be successful. We're going to throw a heavy dose of the running game at them, and we're going to take them out of those pressure packages."

I just wanted to know going into the game what it was that we were going to do. I didn't want any surprises. I didn't want to go into a game not knowing what the play calling was going to be like. I think the coordinators I played for in Dallas were very, very good on Saturday night.

You'd get a sense during the week, too, of what plays the coaches were going to call on Sunday. I never wanted to go into a game thinking we were going to pass, but then the passing game struggles a little bit early, right away we're trying to change our approach from the week of practice. That didn't happen with our coordinators. We usually had a good plan, and we stayed with it.

And the other thing was that in Dallas, it really didn't matter how many passes that the game plan called for. We all knew that one way or another, we'd get into our running game at some point—and that there would be a heavy dose of it.

Bird's-Eye View

Many offensive coordinators (and a few defensive coordinators) prefer to sit in a booth in the press box and communicate to the sidelines via headset. The bird's-eye view gives them the opportunity to see what formations or schemes the opponent is utilizing and how best to counter them. The best coordinators can make subtle adjustments to the game plan or route combinations or blitz packages. Other coordinators like to be on the sidelines. They feel it is more important to talk directly to their players as opposed to communicating via the headset. They will have an assistant in the booth relaying what he sees from his perspective.

Moose's Memories

Norv Turner

Norv Turner was the offensive coordinator in Dallas from 1991 to 1993. We won the Super Bowl each of the last two seasons he ran the offense. Norv always wanted that big-time running back. When he was the offensive coordinator in Dallas, he had Emmitt Smith. When he went to Washington to become the head coach, he had Stephen Davis. Then as the coordinator in Miami, he had Ricky Williams. Now that he's in Oakland as the head coach, he needs to find that running back—the Raiders signed LaMont Jordan, who had been a backup to Curtis Martin for the New York Jets, as a free agent this season, so maybe he'll end up being that guy—because he wants to run the ball thirty to thirty-five times a game in order to open up the passing game. Norv's passing game is a big-play attack as much as it is a ball-control passing game. He utilizes a lot of underneath routes, but he also likes to take shots down the field. Norv's offense in Dallas was perfect for the personnel there. Emmitt Smith could pound the ball when we wanted to, or we could go over the top with Troy Aikman throwing to wide receivers Michael Irvin or Alvin Harper.

That offense was a system similar to what San Diego ran under head coach Don Coryell in the late 1970s and early 1980s. A lot of NFL teams run a version of the West Coast Offense that Paul Brown started in Cincinnati and Bill Walsh popularized in San Francisco (and that was tweaked in Green Bay and Philadelphia). But ours wasn't like that. It was the "Air Coryell" offense that the Chargers ran with Dan Fouts, Chuck Muncie, Kellen Winslow, Charlie Joiner, and John Jefferson.

An offensive coordinator may notice, for instance, that the defense is in a different pass coverage than you expected given the route combinations you've planned, so you adjust. They may call down to the sidelines and tell a Michael Irvin or an Alvin Harper, "Instead of running 7-8-9 today, we want to change it up to 7-8-7 because they're not even playing the corner route on the back side. They're too worried about Alvin going over the top and catching the long pass." Or they might adjust to a 7-8-5, having Alvin come off the ball like he's running the go route the defense is afraid of, only to have him cut it off on a comeback route.

Here's another example: Let's say the defense had zone coverage against the Cowboys. Well, quarterback Troy Aikman was really good at being patient, taking what the defense was giving him, and working all the underneath stuff. That would force the defense to start coming up and playing those routes a little more honestly. Then all of a sudden, he could send tight end Jay Novacek to the second tier on a deeper route.

You can make some really good in-game adjustments from the press box.

Meeting with Coaches

As television analysts, we get to talk with coaches all over the league in our meetings on the Friday and Saturday before a telecast. (We meet with the home team's coaches on Friday and the visiting team's coaches on Saturday.) Just like anyone else, some coaches give you more insight into what they are doing than others. Some guys are more open. Sometimes they'll tell us things that they want off the record. It's all about building trust and about becoming familiar with the teams you work with most.

I've always felt it's important not to waste their time. If you've got a question you want to ask, ask it, get your answer, and let the coaches get back to their work. Their number one priority is to get their team ready for the game, not to meet with you.

I have worked with the Philadelphia Eagles more than any other team as a broadcaster. Eagles head coach Andy Reid is one of my favorite coaches in the NFL, and I actually feel like I have been accepted by Eagle fans . . . yeah, right!

He's Got Personality

A lot of teams will take on the personality of their head coach. A tough, no-nonsense coach like Vince Lombardi had tough, no-nonsense teams. An offensive-minded coach is going to have an offensive-minded team. And a team with a defensive-minded coach likely is going to wind up being strong on that side of the ball.

But one of the important considerations to watch for in today's game is how well a team responds to adversity. And often, you'll see a team takes its lead in that area from its head coach. Look at Atlanta last year. One of the things new coach Jim Mora stressed over and over to his team in his first year was the importance of winning the next down. If something bad happened one play ago or one quarter ago, forget it—that's in the past. There's nothing you can do about it now, so stay focused on that next snap of the ball. Win the next down. Atlanta did that. The Falcons were one of the best teams in the league at responding to adversity—that is, responding when things don't go as planned—and they advanced all the way to the NFC Championship game.

Going for It

One of the most important decisions a coach has to make in the course of a game is whether or not to go for it on fourth down. In most cases, of course, it's a no-brainer. The distance needed for a first down, field position, game score, or other circumstances usually make it an easy call.

But every once in a while the decision rests squarely on the head coach's shoulders. Maybe the offense has moved close to the goal line and doesn't want to settle for a field goal and give the defense a sigh of relief. Maybe the team is in that gray area around the opponent's 35 yard line, where a field goal is an iffy thing and there aren't a lot of yards to be gained by punting. Or maybe the coach just feels a need to give his team a shot in the arm.

Whatever the situation, if it's fourth and short, the home crowd is sure to be chanting, "Go! Go! Go!" but if the gamble doesn't work, it's the head coach who has to shoulder the responsibility.

Sometimes, as a fan, you can accuse your offense of being a little too conservative, but one of the key considerations for a coach on fourth and short is his defense. That might not sound right—you might think that it has more to do with a coach's confidence in his offense. But if a coach knows that he can rely on his defense to stop the opponent, it frees him up to make the decision to go for it. Because then, even if you go for it on fourth down and fail, so what? He knows his defense will go and do its job, and the offense will still get another chance. Sometimes, too, if you're playing at home and the decision is touchdown or field goal, a field goal will take your crowd out of it—even if it's good. But going for it on fourth down keeps the crowd going—even if it fails—because it was a gutsy call. Many people feel that when you are at home, take the points. Kick the field goal and get your three points. I say be aggressive, keep your crowd in the game and maintain the home-field advantage.

A gutsy call only becomes a bad call if you fail and then the defense fails, too, and allows the opposing offense to regain control of the momentum.

Taking the field at Candlestick Park for the NFC Championship game on January 17, 1993. We played one of our best games of that era, beating the 49ers 30–20 and advancing to Super Bowl XXVII.

Photo by Ron St. Angelo

PART EIGHT

The Mental
Game

Troy Aikman, Mark Stepnoski, and I were the first three picks in Jimmy Johnson's first draft class. Not one of us thought we would be riding through the streets of downtown Dallas for a Super Bowl parade three years after our 1–15 rookie campaign.

CHAPTER TWENTY-SEVEN

It's All in Your Head

Time to Retire?

If you can't get ready mentally for a new season, then you know it's time to step away. But what the parameters are for getting ready is going to vary from player to player. For me, I knew that I was ready for the season when I could squat the proper amount in the weight room.

After I injured my neck in 1997, retirement was in the back of my mind more than I ever was ready to admit. By late in my career, I'd watch myself on tape, and I could see that I wasn't playing the same. The neck injury limited my ability to do squats because the bar rested on my back and shoulders. While that's physical, it meant that mentally I wasn't ready because now there was doubt in my mind.

I had been hurt at various times earlier in my career, but those were pain-related issues, which I could deal with. But the neck injury was different. When I first injured my neck and had to stop some of my lower-body strength training, especially the squats, I was a different player from then on. You can do a lot of things with various weight machines, and you can keep your glutes and hamstrings strong and all that, but having the ability and core strength to step out into space carrying all that weight—well, to me, stepping off that rack with 500 pounds on my back and doing reps, in my mind that meant I was ready to play. When I did that, then I knew, "Okay, it's time to go. I'm ready to play." And once I couldn't do that, the doubt crept in. I thought, "What do I do now? How do I know that I'm strong enough to take that defender out of the hole for the running back?"

Then I could see that there were more stalemates on my lead

blocking. And in a stalemate the defender beats me. He wins. It means he did a good job because my running back has nowhere to go. That's when I knew it was time to retire.

Goals

I never was much of a goal setter during my playing career. Just don't get hurt—that was what I wanted from every season. Let me stay relatively healthy all year long, and the rest will take care of itself. I would always say a little prayer before every game, and that's all I asked. "Father, please keep me healthy so I can use the ability that You blessed me with to help this team earn a victory." And that was it. Short and sweet.

It's funny, because when I give motivational talks now, that's one of the things that I stress—to set goals and to keep focused on them. But I never really set any specific goals as a player. Oh, sure, after I caught 50 passes in 1993, I thought it would be great to catch 50 again, that sort of thing. But I was always a team-oriented player. I never really knew what goals to set for myself. Because the only real goal was winning a championship. Anything else was just icing on the cake.

Preparing for the Season

Preparing for the coming season is year-round now, and it's very rigorous. In Dallas we were back working out about four or five weeks after our last game. We were in the Super Bowl several years at the end of January, then I went to the Pro Bowl a couple of times the first week of February, so by March 1 or March 7 or so, I was back at it.

A player starts building gradually for the upcoming season—it's a progression through the entire off-season. The first six-week period is about building a foundation. Strength training includes higher reps with lower weights, and conditioning starts with longer distances or more time on cardiovascular machines. This takes a player right up to about the time of the NFL draft in late April.

After all the veterans have gone through the initial phase, the new guys come in for minicamp. This continues the progression. Strength training becomes medium reps with moderate weights. Speed training and explosive work (plyometrics, Olympic lifting) are started, and conditioning is geared toward the conditioning test you will run before camp. For us in Dallas it was usually sixteen 110-yard sprints completed in specific times (15, 17, or 19 seconds depending on your position) with a 45-second recovery between them.

About the beginning of June, there's another minicamp. Then a big push until the beginning of July. The final phase becomes very football specific. Strength training with low reps and higher weights. Speed training, explosive exercises, and conditioning continue. Field drills and metabolic conditioning are added. Metabolics are position-specific field drills done in three to six groups of ten with timed recoveries. Finally, a few days off and training camp starts. Whew.

Daryl congratulates former teammate Emmitt Smith, who in 2002 had just established a new NFL rushing record.   Photos courtesy Fox Sports

History Book

One collective goal we all did have on the Cowboys offense was to help Emmitt Smith win rushing titles. He achieved his first of four titles in 1991. I'm not sure any of us besides Emmitt thought he would become the NFL's all-time leading rusher, but he still holds the title by more than 1,600 yards over Walter Payton.

After the Cowboys Emmitt went on to play for the Arizona Cardinals for two years beginning in 2003. He finished his career with a strong 2004 season in which he rushed for 937 yards and 9 touchdowns. At the end of the year, he retired with a league-record 18,355 rushing yards in fifteen NFL seasons.

The Fox Sports broadcast team takes advantage of some downtime to visit the White House: (left to right) Bob Stenner, Dick Stockton, Sandy Grossman, and Daryl.

Photo courtesy Daryl Johnston

CHAPTER TWENTY-EIGHT

Life after Football

Preparing for a Career Off the Field

In 1997 I was seriously hurt for the first time—I had surgery that October to fuse two vertebrae in my neck. And during the slow week between the conference championship games that season and before the competing teams got to the Super Bowl city, a rumor circulated that I was retiring. So I got some inquiries from the networks: What was I going to do? Would I be interested in coming down for an audition to do some game analysis? I said thanks, but no thanks. I appreciated their interest, but I intended to get back on the field and play again. The second time I got hurt, in 1999, I called them!

I had the opportunity to do a lot of television and radio work during my playing career in Dallas, so I had some experience before my playing days were over. Plus, we had so much media here for every practice and after games. It's basically just repetition—just like everything else, the more you do it, the easier it gets.

I had a lot of practice with broadcasting, a lot of on-the-job training. I had a radio show when I was a player. Near the end of my career, I had a morning drive segment called "Moose Calls" on a local radio station.

While I had a lot of opportunities, I never really thought, "Hey, let me use these as a vehicle to practice for later." I just enjoyed doing it. It was a lot of fun, and there were financial benefits.

Moose's Memories

People always ask what I would have done if I hadn't played professional football. I was an economics major at Syracuse and really enjoyed international economics and banking. I probably would have looked into something that combined the two. But who can ever know?

I certainly didn't have any idea that I would wind up in broadcasting. The Newhouse School at Syracuse is a very famous broadcasting school, but I would have had to have known coming out of high school that that's what I wanted to do. The Newhouse School is very difficult to get into, and then if you don't get in as a freshman, the transfer requirements are even higher than the admission standards.

My Latest Role

One of the things that I really enjoyed during my playing career was hearing the fans cheer for me, hearing them call "Mooooose!" every time I touched the ball, because it showed that they looked beyond the statistics to appreciate a guy for the behind-the-scenes work that he was doing, for being part of a team and doing whatever it takes to win. Heck, I didn't even run for 1,000 yards in my eleven seasons in the league. Emmitt Smith would reach that in less than eleven games.

I'm no longer with the Cowboys, but I'm still part of a team—the broadcasting team at Fox. And I'm still willing to do whatever behind-the-scenes work that it takes to make this team a success.

Preparing for a Telecast

When I prepare for a telecast, it's a full week obligation—maybe an hour and a half or a couple of hours each day. That's not nearly the amount of time that I spent preparing for a game as a player, but it's more than I expected to be doing coming into broadcasting.

In fact, during the first year, I overprepared for the telecasts. Then it became a matter of finding that comfort zone between what's not enough preparation and what is too much preparation. I didn't want to go overboard so that I couldn't react properly to what was happening during the game. I didn't want my mind cluttered with all this information that I'd gathered during the course of the week so that I couldn't think clearly on game day or explain what was happening on the field.

A Broadcaster's Week

I get files every day. Starting on a Monday, I get local sports pages from the cities of the teams that we're going to do. That gives me a general idea of what's going on and what people are thinking. I don't want to go into a production meeting later in the week and ask a question that I should have had the answer to on Tuesday afternoon. I want to be prepared, and I want to ask educated questions when I sit down with the coaches and players.

I watch game tapes a couple of days a week here in Dallas, and I watch them just as I did when I was a player. Then I start digging a little deeper—make a couple of calls to get a little bit of inside information. Then it's back to the tapes to see if they validate what I've learned, or if there are more questions I need to ask.

We need to be at the home team's practice on the Friday before the game. We'll watch practice and just kind of talk informally among ourselves, then we talk to the players and coaches with whom we've requested meetings. Then I go back to the hotel and watch some more film on the laptop that I bring along on the weekends.

There's a production dinner on Friday night at which we bounce some ideas off each other. It's not a lot of work, really, but it's a great way of building camaraderie. Dick Stockton (the play-by-play man) and I spend a lot of time with each other during the weekend and just talk about things. And as a group, Bob Stenner (the producer), Sandy Grossman (the director), Dick, and I might go for a walk on Saturday morning and get in a little bit of a workout.

After that I start to get all the notes from the home team organized on my board, which has all the players' names and numbers and positions for reference during the broadcasts. Then we start working on any follow-up questions for the home team that may have arisen, or those that we want to ask the visiting team, which comes in on

Saturday. We have our meeting with the visiting team and go back to the hotel. There's a production meeting for the crew on Saturday night, but before that there's time to get notes organized and put the visiting team's info on the board. At the production meeting we view any new or special graphics or video clips that will be utilized during the telecasts. We also go over any other information that's come up, and Tony Siragusa provides his perspective on the game. Tony has good insight into parts of the game that I am unsure of because of his defensive background.

So it's a lot like the schedule for a player. Everything is slotted in and scheduled to build up to game time on Sunday—it's just not nearly as time intensive.

Film Study

As a player, I spent a lot of time in the film room—studying the opposing team's tendencies and the players I would go up against—and I still do. I always watch a tape of our game, and of our segment on the pregame show, and I grade myself. Am I talking too fast? Saying stupid things?

We get the broadcast films of other games sent to us, too. If we have Seattle and Atlanta coming up, I'll get Seattle's and Arizona's games from the previous week. I can watch those telecasts, but I don't really ever do that. I go straight to the game film—the coaches' film, which has the end-zone and sideline cuts that I used to watch as a player.

I find that film study helps my producer and my director, too. We talk it through, and it gives them a heads-up as to where my eyes are going to be. If a team breaks the huddle in a certain formation, they know what I'm looking at and can adjust accordingly. Or I might tell them by the formation what I'm expecting to see, and they can be sure to have a camera on the right players.

Broadcasting Philosophy

Our philosophy on the telecasts is, "Don't get in the way of the game." I'm smart enough to know that people are tuning in to watch the game, not to listen to me. So I don't want to get in the way. The last thing I want is for them to turn down the sound on the television and turn up the volume on the local radio station.

I pick and choose what I try to teach the audience because there is so little time during the course of a broadcast to really get into any situation in depth. And then not only to get into it in depth, but also to explain it in layman's terms and make it easy for everyone to understand.

So, if I see something one week that I feel is going to be a predominate part of the game, I try to focus on that, then wait for an opportunity during the broadcast to break it down and talk about it. But those opportunities are hard to come by.

Sometimes something will jump out at you all of a sudden during the course of a game, whether it was part of your old offense, something you know from playing a particular opponent in the past, or something you know about a coach's philosophy from having talked with him over the years. When those things come up, you jump on it.

Feedback

I have a few friends, just fans of football, whose opinions matter a lot to me, and who give me feedback. And I've had people in Dallas stop me and say they really enjoy the telecasts, that they're different.

What I like best is when they say, "I really like your style." Because it *is* different. The thing that we have done—Dick Stockton and Tony Siragusa, my broadcast partners, and I—is moved in a little bit of a different direction on how we cover the game. Our style is more conversational than most. We break down the plays during our game and do some work concerning the Xs and Os, but we also take a step back to see how this fits into the overall flow of the game. We then expand that into a big picture view of the teams' division, progressing to the conference level and the overall impact on the NFL. We attempt to look at the impact the game will have not only from the results that day but what happens as the season progresses in the weeks to come.

I think today's fan is educated enough about the game of football that he or she can watch a broadcast and have a reasonable idea of what happened or why someone did something. So I hope to find an opportunity to take them into an area that they're not sure about. Maybe explain something to them that they didn't know. And then, as I said at the beginning of this book, when I'm finished with the telecast, I hope the viewers will feel that they learned a few things. Just as I hope you have with this book.

It's hard not to be successful when you have guys like quarterback Troy Aikman (8) and running back Emmitt Smith (22) on your team.

Photo by Ron St. Angelo

WATCHING FOOTBALL

Daryl Johnston's Career Statistics

Fullback

6'2", 238 pounds

Born: February 10, 1966, Youngstown, NY

High School: Lewiston-Porter (Youngstown, NY)

College: Syracuse University

Drafted: 1989, 2nd round (Dallas)

Year	Rushing				Receiving			
	Att	Yds	Avg	TD	No	Yds	Avg	TD
1989	67	212	3.2	0	16	133	8.3	3
1990	10	35	3.5	1	14	148	10.6	1
1991	17	54	3.2	0	28	244	8.7	1
1992	17	61	3.6	0	32	249	7.8	2
1993	24	74	3.1	3	50	372	7.4	1
1994	40	138	3.5	2	44	325	7.4	2
1995	25	111	4.4	2	30	248	8.3	1
1996	22	48	2.2	0	43	278	6.5	1
1997	2	3	1.5	0	18	166	9.2	1
1998	8	17	2.1	0	18	60	3.3	1
1999	0	0	0	0	1	4	4.0	0
Totals	232	753	3.2	8	294	2,227	7.6	14

Daryl's Career Highlights

- Played in 149 consecutive games from 1989 to 1997

- Selected for the Pro Bowl in the 1993 and 1994 seasons

- Played on three Super Bowl championship teams in Dallas: 1992 (Super Bowl XXVII), 1993 (XXVIII), and 1995 (XXX)

- As the lead blocker, helped pave the way for teammate Emmitt Smith to lead the NFL in rushing four times in five seasons from 1991 to 1995

Index

Cunningham, Richie, 179
cut blocks, 94–95

D

Dallas Cowboys. *See also specific
personnel names*
 "America's Team," 3
 defense, 124, 125
 "down by contact" dispute, 52
 field size discrepancy, 14
 game plans, 213–14
 passing plays, 68
 play calling, 66–67, 70
 Super Bowl memories, 16, 21,
 30, 68, 175, 205
 team chemistry, 41
 Thanksgiving Day, 204
 tight end receptions, 104
 uniforms, 26
 weather affecting, 31
Davis, Stephen, 215
Dawkins, Brian, 79, 131
Dayne, Ron, 144
defense
 best players, 131
 blitzes, 45, 79–80, 143, 147
 communication on, 138–39
 defined/purpose of, 8
 dictating tempo, 124–25
 famous unit nicknames, 125
 great players, 124, 127, 131
 importance of, 123–25
 levels, 71
 Moose's memories, 123, 130
 passive vs. aggressive, 124–25
 positions on. *See* defensive
 positions
 quarterbacks reading, 79–81
 stunts, 118, 152–54

 of wide receivers, 105–6
 winning championships
 with, 123
 zone blitz, 79–80
 zone vs. man-for-man
 protection, 116
defenses (base), 133–39
 defined, 133
 4-3 defense, 126, 128,
 133–35, 151
 46 defense, 135–38
 3-4 defense, 126, 128, 129,
 133–35
 when to use, 133
defenses (pass). *See* pass coverages
defenses (run), 141–45
 changing pace, 144–45
 eight-man fronts, 143–44
 filling gaps, 142–43
 key to, 141
 making tackles, 141–42
 safeties supporting, 142–43
 as top priority, 141
defensive holding, 148
defensive positions, 97, 126–31
 backs (secondary), 130–31
 cornerbacks, 130–31, 152
 ends, 128–29
 linebackers, 126–27
 linemen, 128–29, 141–42
 making tackles and, 141–42
 noseguards (tackles), 128, 129
 run defense and, 141–45
 safeties, 130–31, 142–43, 148
 tackles, 128, 129
delay of game signal, 56
Dempsey, Tom, 182
Dent, Richard, 136
Detmer, Koy, 73

interceptions, defined, 9
international growth, 5
"in the slot," 69
Irvin, Michael, 76, 97, 103, 105,
   106, 215, 216

J

James, Edgerrin, 70, 71
Jansen, Jon, 113
Jefferson, John, 215
Johnson, Jimmy, 194, 201–2, 209
Johnson, Ted, 100
Johnston, Daryl "Moose"
   autograph seekers and, 196–97
   broadcasting philosophy,
      230–32
   career development, 193–94,
      227–32
   career statistics/highlights,
      233–34
   coaches of, 209
   dealing with fans, 196–97
   goals, 224
   injuries/retirement,
      223–24, 227
   Moose's memories. *See specific*
      topics
   nickname origin, 193
   number of, 27
   off-field career, 227–32
   preparing for telecast, 228–29
Joiner, Charlie, 215
Jones, Deacon, 125
Jones, Jerry, 194
Jones, Walter, 201
Jordan, LaMont, 215
Joyner, Seth, 101

K

Kansas City Chiefs, 11, 21,
   116, 165
K-ball, 179
Kearse, Jevon, 114, 128, 154
Kelly, Jim, 78
kicking game. *See* field goals/extra
   points; kickoffs; special teams
kickoffs, 167–71
   anticipating direction of, 168
   covering, 168–70
   onside kicks, 47, 170–72
   returning, 185–87
   strategies for, 167–68
   yard line for, 167
kick protection, 182
Kiffin, Monte, 142
Kiick, Jim, 193
Killer B's, 125
Kilmer, Billy, 85
Knapp, Greg, 37
Kosar, Bernie, 83, 196

L

Lambert, Jack, 124
Landeta, Sean, 173
Landry, Tom, 151, 193
Laufenberg, Babe, 193
Leaf, Ryan, 73
Lechler, Shane, 174
Leftwich, Byron, 87
length of games. *See* timing of
   games
Lett, Leon, 31
Lewis, Chad, 83
Lewis, Jamal, 112
Lewis, Marvin, 134
Lewis, Ray, 41, 126, 127, 131,
   139, 141

Shotgun Offense, 84–85
spying, 156–57
synchronizing with receivers, 81–82, 83
two-minute drill, 85–87
Quarter Halves defense, 80
quarters, 10
Quarters defense, 80

R

Ramsey, Patrick, 75–76
Randle, John, 129
Ratterman, George, 26
receivers. *See also* wide receivers
    giving 100% every play, 106
    ineligible, 114
    Moose's memories, 105, 107
    route accuracy, 107
    tight ends, 103–4
red zone, 48, 84
Reed, Ed, 41, 131
Reed, J. R., 186
referees
    roles of, 54
    signals of, 56–57, 65
replay challenges, 53–54
retirement, 223–24
returns
    free kicks on, 189
    kickoff, 185–87
    punt, 187–89
RFK Stadium, 21
Rhodes, Ray, 147
Rice, Jerry, 105, 106
Rice, Simeon, 128
Roethlisberger, Ben, 64
Rose Bowl, 21
roughing the quarterback, 88
running backs, 91–101

avoiding big hits, 93–94
blocking by, 98, 99–100
blocking for, 94–96
catching passes, 96–98, 99
changing pace with, 144–45
defending. *See* defenses (run)
fullbacks, 98–99
great players, 92–93
halfbacks, 91
H-backs, 91
line injuries affecting, 113
mental game for, 94
Moose's memories, 92, 97, 100, 101
positions, 91
presnap reads by, 93
running routes, 99
skills of, 91
running plays, 70–71
Ryan, Buddy, 125, 135, 136, 137

S

sack, 48
safeties (points), 7
safeties (positions), 130–31, 142, 148
Samuels, Chris, 113
Sanders, Barry, 93, 107
Sanders, Deion, 131, 188
San Diego Chargers, 215
San Francisco 49ers, 68, 85
Sapp, Warren, 129, 142
Saxon, Mike, 175, 189
scheme, 48
scoring, 7
scramble drill, 88–89
scrimmage line, 47
seam, 48
season, preparing for, 224–25

About the Authors

After **Daryl "Moose" Johnston** earned the respect and admiration of his teammates for his contributions to the Dallas offense, he received national recognition for his play in 1993 when he became the first blocking fullback selected to the NFC Pro Bowl team. As the lead blocker for the Cowboys, he helped pave the way for Emmitt Smith to win four NFL rushing titles, and he helped Dallas win three Super Bowls in the 1990s.

Johnston played eleven seasons in Dallas before a neck injury originally suffered in 1997 led to his retirement after the 1999 season. He immediately became a star analyst in the broadcast booth, first for CBS and, since 2001, for Fox.

Daryl earned a bachelor's degree in economics from Syracuse and is a leading advocate for literacy initiatives. He lives in Texas with his wife and two children.

Jim Gigliotti spent eleven years with the NFL's publishing division before becoming a freelance writer and editor. Recent writing credits include *Stadium Stories: USC Trojans* and children's and young adult books on numerous subjects, including NASCAR, the NBA, Major League Baseball, and sports in America. He lives in Southern California with his wife and two children.

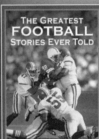

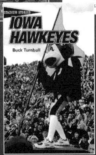